Kentucky Review
2014

Editor-in-Chief
Robert S. King

Associate Editors
Joan Colby, Mike James, Helen Losse

www.kentuckyreview.org

A Good Works Project

ISSN 2376-9920 (print)
ISSN 2376-9939 (online)

Cover artwork, "Sober Landscape," by Fons Heijnsbroek
Cover and interior book design by Diane Kistner
Charter text with Insignia titling

Published by Kentucky Review (a division of FutureCycle Press)
Lexington, Kentucky, USA

ISSN 2376-9920
ISBN 978-1-938853-88-3

FORWARD

On behalf of the Associate Editors Joan Colby, Helen Losse, and Mike James, I am proud to offer our first printed edition of *Kentucky Review*.

Founded in 2014, *KR* published nearly 100 poets online in its first year. This printed edition is a compilation of all of the poems posted on the website during 2014. We intend to produce a print edition each year in January containing the previous year's work from the website.

Although based in Lexington, Kentucky, *KR* has no regional focus and publishes English-language works from around the world. I will not bore you with a long, lofty mission statement. We editors have but one goal: to publish work we like. Hopefully, the contents of this issue will show that our tastes are eclectic as long as the writing is good.

The first issue of *KR* is limited to poetry. Starting January 1, 2015, however, we will begin publishing flash fiction as well. Poets in this issue appear in alphabetical order by last name with author bios at the end. Please visit www.kentuckyreview.org for author photos, submission guidelines, and new work published online throughout the coming year. If you like what you read here, we hope you'll post comments on the work you enjoyed.

I wish to thank the editors for their diligence and professionalism in evaluating submissions. I also thank Diane Kistner, Director of FutureCycle Press, for her book design skills. And to all whose poems appear in this issue, we appreciate your contributions. As the saying goes, "it takes a village...."

—Robert S. King, Editor-in-Chief

IN THIS ISSUE

Coastal Autumn at Sandy Hook

The strand unfolds before me in the blue swell
of flanking ocean, the mute passage of light.

I come upon amaranth blossoms, plovers, sea glass
gathering its worn grace. Dark birds slide their hunger

above sand that grows rich with the broken splendor
of whelks and slipper shells—the quiet exit

of their small lives. A man approaches the shoreline
alone, suddenly turns back as if he'd misidentified

the sea, or come for nothing more than a lone
tanker that wayfares the far reach of the world.

I fix on a kite's florid streamers, suspended
like a wish above the child that flew it, till a mist

comes landward off the Atlantic surf like a dissolving
ghost, and I turn to leave the strand,

some thought left vague at the edge of recall,
like a hand I had somewhere forgotten to grasp.

JEFFREY ALFIER

Toward Winter on Woodgate Avenue

Late day, and from a radio set on a window
ledge, chamber music I can't name wavers
over my parent's lawn, its weather-beaten trees.
Wind searches trellis, trap, wicker chair and windfall.
The day is a dusty page torn from the calendar.

Standing in the back doorway, I'm called out
of this fall daydream, leaves brushing my feet
like a losing hand of cards flung by a failed gambler.
My father is at his garden, cursing deer that come
to take unoffered tithes of year-end crops. Angry,
his boots collapse a tunnel dug by animal hunger.

At the end of his days, he wants his ashes strewn
over some river up north, perhaps the Willimantic,
namesake of his birth town. As I watch him, he paces
over the lawn to the vine-thralled fence I helped
build, decades ago. His steps are a timeless trooping
to the beat of shears and shovel, leaves clocking
down around him, slow, the sunlight like smoke.

JEFFREY ALFIER

Artesia Boulevard Story

Redondo Beach, California

Somewhere between the claw hammer
I bought on sale from Kurt's True Value
and the Shell station coffee and 7-11
hot wings now burning my gut, this cool
November morning ascends the bric-a-brac
mothball and tobacco air of the Goodwill
I exit, a stuffed Santa slumping like a drunk
in the corner of its storefront window.
I pass Mexican landscapers taking their break
of Gatorade and tacos in the shade
of Pep Boys auto. A drunk on a bus stop
bench wants to show me in his slurred
lexicon a card trick he calls three card monte.

But I pass his offer up, hope against hope
the door of Bac Street Lounge is unlocked,
its marquee wishing someone named
Ashley a Happy Birthday. But luck won't answer
my tug at the door, resistance saying come back
later, this street I may or may not return
to after dark, its neon like mascara bleeding over
sidewalks under the cold rind of the waning
moon, the last clerk, locking up Goodwill,
blowing a tired cloud of smoke that rides
her breath like sparrows through the dark.

Pie Filling

Sipping my morning coffee
I crave a slice of your pie,
the ones made from green
apples you'd let me select
from a roadside fruit stand,
in the autumn crisp.

You once told me.
when I dropped one to the floor,
bruises add flavor and scars
build character, we merely need
to spoon a little sugar and nutmeg.

The children will stir soon.
I'll pack an apple in each lunch bag,
help them button their overcoats,
tucking in enough warmth
to last the day. I remember how
you'd crimp the edges of pie dough,
careful to seal in your love.

Mapping His Freckles

He smells like peanut butter
mixed with adolescent sweat, his
palms wet as he takes your hand,
escorting you in secret to his favorite
corner in the library.

"When I grow up" he boasts "there will be
books with orange covers, written about my life,
displayed here, next to *Eli: Boy Mechanic* and
Abe: Frontier Boy."

And you can't help but wish your book report
due next week wasn't about Clara Barton and
her Red Cross, but instead Matt Redman and
his Red Hair. Perhaps even a map of his freckles
for extra credit.

You can't resist poking your finger through
the hole in his blue jeans, tickling his knee,
his laughter catching a snarl from the librarian,
a brief pause in the rhythmic pounding of her
stamp-to-stamp-pad, inking revised due dates
on a stack of index cards.

And someday you'll ponder, while making
PB&J's for your own children, if anyone ever
discovered the love notes you hid for each other
in the card catalog, under *biographies,*
wondering if he ever read your last note
before moving away to a new school.

The Unfinished

a cento

Framed in her phoenix fire-screen, Edna Ward
bends to the tray of Canton, pouring tea
where light breaks and windows are tossed with linden.

The poem unwritten, left in her mind undone, the years
a forest of giant stones, of fossil stumps, blocking the altar.
Nouns were clustered in the street, stuck, changed.
An adjective walked by. A verb drove up. In the springtime,
the sentences and the nouns lay silently on the grass.

> *Young as I am, old as I am, the bud stands for all things,*
> *even for those things that don't flower. My swirling wants.*
> *Your frozen lips. The grammar that turned and attacked me.*

The classics can console. But not enough—wind chimes off-key
in the alcove. We were characters in a story the writer
couldn't bring himself to finish.
Edna Ward bends to the tray of Canton, pouring tea.

Title:
Laurie Sheck

First Stanza:
first two lines—"Cottage Street," 1953, Richard Wilbur
third line—"The Writer," Richard Wilbur

Second stanza:
first two lines—"The Poem Unwritten," Denise Levertov
Next three lines—"Permanently," Kenneth Koch

Third Stanza:
first part of line one—"Air," W.S. Merwin
second half and 3/4thof next line—"Saint Francis and the Sow," Galway Kinell
rest of second line and third line—"A Valediction Forbidding Mourning," Adrienne Rich

Fourth Stanza:
first line—"Sea Grapes," Derek Walcott
wind chime line—"Black Silk," Tess Gallagher
second and third line—"The Unfinished," Laurie Sheck
last line—"Cottage Street," 1953, Richard Wilbur

When I Think of You

the sheen of silver stills the sea, and my dread swims
to the surface. You stroke out of your depth.

Can we find a language without our own fears in it?
The dark green heralds the rain before it begins, the strange light.

We lay together face to face, our love holding hands between us.
Your body abandoning you, raging, calling out.

Remember, love, the vineyard, the sun-filled grapes and tightened skins,
the wine from them we drank in Provence, the bird reinventing his song?

When I think of you, my love, I will recall what remains—
flashes of orange, stellar blue and the fire-red breast.

A Song on the End

First there will be your darkening heart
beating against misleading light
as if startled by shellfire.
You will burn like opening breath,
contain fire without flinching.
As birds remember snow
under a column of sky, you
will remember the feel of the path.
Sixty years to the coast,
it's easy as whistling.

The Joy of Cooking

Tear down the walls
of your kitchen,
wear your apron tied
tight to hide the condiments
of rapture. Capture the wide
face of the moon
in your largest pot. Gather
the recollection of sunlight
upon the shoulders of young women.
There is no death when our teeth
crunch chicken bones, when our tongues
are slicked with yellow fat.
There is no death
when we lick our sticky lips.
There is love in milk
and salvation in the butter of heaven.

Elegy for My Mother

It seemed she was always standing
between the door and the west moon,
wearing a soiled shirt and old shoes.
Rusted rasps and chisels, the calendar
with notes scribbled
in her diminished hand,
the fragile vehicle of her skull,
that ruined house,
entirely too large for what was left.
Eleven years she has been ashes
spun where stones lie in the sun
on Mohawk Hill.
She left me a key, I think.

Surviving the 1970s

I owe apologies
to the ghosts

of the none-too-few
crawdads a boy
I knew plucked out

of the creek
down in the holler
behind his granny's house

to tear tail
from claw in the name
of something

the opposite
of true science
except that he/I was

more of a textbook case
than most.

Nobody saw me
commit
these crimes

bare handed
watery eyed
heaving air

but I was well
aware my fingerprints
were all over

those damn weeds
I'd flung full
of guts

theirs or mine
or God's I couldn't tell.

What an
awkward time
that was

finding my way
through the dark woods
and back uphill

into the bright
hot afternoons

crawling blindly
on my hands
and knees

done for good I thought
as a killer.

Dandelions

Golden dandelions
linger carelessly by the roadside;
hitchhikers thumbing for a ride.
Their lemon yellow petals
peppering the earth with fallen sunshine.
The painted honey hills melt
like objects in a Dali painting
onto the dried apricot landscape,
home to gophers, coyote, and rattlesnakes.
Days drive by like fast cars,
leaving black tread marks
on cracked roads headed somewhere
the sun is a different hue of happy.
The elder dandelions wait in the distance
for that pacific breeze, feathery light
that will take them away;
scattering pieces of themselves
white and transparent
toward some semblance of Heaven.

Blanket

We never thought we'd end up here,
sweeping endless prairie dust
off our front porch.
In the evening, as we sleep,
the intrusive wind taps
our window panes,
reminding us of the antelope
and deer
ever grazing on lost time.

You say the stray tumbleweed
reminds you of me;
I don't take offense. I know you.
How the truth unfolds delicately
from your mother's nurturing arms.

Do you glimpse colors of her in me?

Is that the reason you've stayed
all these years,
holding my hand tightly in yours.
Fingers and gold bands woven together
like a blanket of sturdy bones
and curled sunlight.

NANCY BEVILAQUA

Alabastron

(from *Gospel of the Throwaway Daughter*)

This shadow smells of cedar, dust.
Roman horses pass outside, daylight
bleeding from the street. In my mouth
the taste of what is necessary
now, last finger
on the dial of the sun: bridal veil,
widow's vial, something strong
for what's to come.

We dream all this, you say,
but I promise we awaken, and that
will have to be enough: you will not try
to get away.

Lift your hair for me. My fingers
would trail honey down your face,
trace starry figures on your back, but we
are strangers here, and time
runs short, and there are cannibals
who wait. I hear my own words
whispered; we are both open
in this rite. Spikenard's bitter
on your brow. I will spread it
with my hands, somehow
draw you through these moments
so we both come out alive.

BYRON BEYNON

Places

He defines places by their foundations,
their firmness, the strength of roots,

how morning sometimes comes
with a red wound in the tempered east,

the illusion of a new sunshine
arriving within the stillness of a winter's room;

a day toasted by the wine of angels,
secret tears that meet

by the sea's drained heart,
when all tides

escape from this life,
the flotsam sacrificed beneath sharpened steel.

Horses in the Rain

For long hours the horses have stood
in the rain,
in landscapes washed
by a stained canvas of sky,
quenched grass, a bruised green,
they occupy a torso of field
knowing the squall of the day will pass,
the focus of their stare
beyond hedges shaped by the wind;
from the Bucephalus of history
they sense ancestors at wars,
loaded carts and carriages pulled
through mud,
a focus within art,
the racing-reelers of cinema,
each eye haunted by echoes of arid plains
as the jewelled water exudes over them.

Something to Write About

One morning I thought I found it
deep in the vacancy of a ladder.
It had been left leaning oddly
against the steps of my neighbor's
gazebo all night. Other neighbors

spoke softly in the yard, hands
in the air attempting to reenact
something no one witnessed
except those that only alert us
of themselves—cuts in the cedar,

grass bent by the wheels of a stretcher,
a hanging plant growing out of itself,
broken off from the only version
of earth it knew. I've longed for this
kind of occurrence to write about,

to make me feel alive again. I'd been
lost in my own history of change,
condemned by alternate outcomes,
so deep in the silence of my own
stories even the siren that shadowed

my neighbor away couldn't wake me.
I needed the guilt that was slowly
stirring it's invisible ink—the path
just being a path, knowing something
will always be just out of reach.

Seasons

to Chuck

Once again something said it was time
and I couldn't resist some Easter flowers,
the kind I always thought smelled like sex
for some season. When I read hyacinths
require a long, hard winter for the best
results, I knew they were what I missed.

So it was that spring morning waiting for
spring among the roots and ruins I'd left
in shallow graves—the desperate, loose
ends of echoes faithful as my shadow's

face. As for you, Chuck, don't worry
if worry is where you are, she's still your
wife, your name rolls off her tongue like
rain, she waters your white rose every day
with certain sounds—your death lives on
such things. However, only wildflowers

are left of her now and she's promised them
all to me. And I know I should thank you,
if it weren't for you I wouldn't be here
on the side of some road with her. But,

I won't. After another long, hard winter
who knows what comes up again—some
scent, those results. We can't resist when
a cold hand comes warming us, to be
controlled by what's out of control, those
resurrections that daze us as we die on.

Calling

Somewhere sort of sacred inside
I'm an abandoned rural church,
darkened by the figures of stained
glass I've become—you can feel
the prayers I never got around
to pray as they ransack alters after
unattended hours. I'm the priest

that died decades ago, his secrets
still filling the empty choir loft
with the incense of nights alone,
burning off confessions kept
to himself—each day I picture
a different angel listening. Once
the wind finds the bell tower

I flock through freshly painted
doors. In my favorite pew, close
to my softest sins, my back to
guilt, the resistance to follow
someone out of myself appears
as I lean, reach, look in—pass
a vanishing plate to no one.

GEORGE BISHOP

With My Daughter Overseas

I've begun to recognize her on this side
as the photographs come sailing over, late
afternoon and an ocean away. From here
everyone looks like a visitor, even locals,
each sample of creation fully immersed

in some unique and unlimited access
to the arts. She visits a castle, discovers
the rotted posts from a fort-of-herself,
walls she once believed in, partially
died behind as we all must. She stares

at a painting until it's clear she has to
let the painting stare at her if she's to
keep her imaginary brushes dry, allow
the message to mirror a door in her
where nothing's ever been hung. Then,

the stories she's heard can settle, a secret
stranger following her from one to another,
someone walking without bones, leaving
her expressions looking unrehearsed
and gracefully afraid—wine to wine

she writes home with what won't come
home, can't stay. I've begun to recognize her—
stone peering out of statues, clocks set deep
in steeples, her father always looking out
in wonder at all the water, the late hour.

Good Intentions

There were demons in the trees waiting
to drop into our unguarded souls. Words
let them in and words could keep them out
if we would only listen. Some rode in
to our homes on the backs of black cats, squelched
beneath corks, or hidden in the silence
that follows too many questions. The greatest
of them was a fallen singer which reminded us
not to let ourselves be swayed by the rhythms
of the world. Others lorded over flies, putting
any corpse to envy. There were demons
for every sin, and sins for every thought,
all of us cowering in the lights, afraid
the shadows would reach into our hearts
and find themselves at home.

ROSE MARY BOEHM

School Reunion

Fifty years later we meet again.
The 'in'-group found me via the internet.
I travelled all the way from Spain.

Once I was friendly with three or four.
As close as you get when you
bike to school together.

The boys used to wait for us
under the plane trees,
showed off their hands-free skills.

I didn't remember their names,
30 old men and 40 old women,
pot bellies, sparse hair, shapeless

bodies in serious suits, lips cut
across wrinkled faces.
One wheel chair.

I avoided the mirror when I left.
One old man leaned against the fence,
holding his face in his hands.

Compostela was once called the Field of Stars

Starting in St. Jean de Pied
we walked about 20 km, with 780 km
to go. To the center of the greater
pilgrimages.

St. James of Compostela, legend
and shard of transcendent truths.
Take the route of the Milky Way,
he said to Charlemagne.

Occasional sharp morning light
flows over us under the tall trees
of the Pyrenees. Our pace slows.
Pass the water bottles. The cheerless

dirt roads along open fields
seem relentless. 40 more days
at this pace. I hoped it would, but
the hand of God hovers nowhere.

ACE BOGGESS

"Hello Dahling LOL Whatcha Doin?"

—asked by Andrea Fekete (by text message)

I'm tying my shoes much tighter
so my feet don't slip out & dance.
I'm gunning my lips with hot glue
to weigh the corners down.
See that shadow that looks like me?
Over there waving his arm in the air?
I'll slap the grin right off him.
Watch me. See if I won't.
There's too much of the frivolous
binding my arms with daisy chains.
I mean to put an end to it,
to burn down the candy house &
leave the witch. Call me bring-
down, killjoy, curmudgeon.
Try to spike my punch with sunshine.
No, Miss! I'm tired of all this
happiness—the birds
aflutter in my throat,
the steaks on the fire,
the cake in the pan.
Let me rest a moment
before the funeral of despair
begins with jazzy clarinets.
For whom they toll...
Oh, Lord, for whom they toll....

Hit the Ground

This kid I coach
is brave as hell—
against kids three feet bigger,
he sets his body against
lowered shoulders—
awkward pubescent strength—
to be hit, plowed,
exploded from his sneakers.
After he hits the ground,
he's up and grinning,
darting the floor—ninety-four ft.
He quickens the lane,
throws his body up at the goal
when I tell him to.
Play hard. I say. Leave it all
on the court.
He's twelve, concussed again.
His head's the biggest thing on him.
His lip's bloody.
All his rage, confusion, hormones
steaming off the floor.
Like a stupid dog,
he runs against the fence
to retrieve the ball, to obey.

How I envy his innocent belief,
his bald sense of trust.
This, I tell him, is how you should
love a woman,
how you must father a child.
The game can't hurt him enough.

RICHARD BROBST

Feeding Kittens

They make you want to name them
But I don't
Figuring it would be a jinx,
Knowing the odds were already stacked.
Besides, one should not become attached

I remind myself each morning
As they become less concerned
With my movements,
Arch to meet my leg.
But still I am anxious until I count five

Counting at times in the night
The prints of bobcat, fox, coyote,
That prey on the edge of my imagination
As if scenting the corners of ragged shadows.
In truth

I suppose that one might make it,
Grow into full fur,
Find a voice of declaration
And return to lock eyes with me again.
I suppose that one might make it

And so I speak to them all
As if they might remember.

Around the Loop

He can't remember the rabbit
slipping into the hole
so wears slippers
unless I help him dress
on the few days
I make it to see him.
He turns burners off
but forgets sometimes
to turn them on
and laughs that cold soup
reminds him of army days,
eating rocks off the Italian coast.
He can still shave
badly. He can go days
without talking with me
but can't stop talking
if a young person sits
near his electrically perfected
ear. He is happy with Nascar
and the leftist revolutions
going on for hours
and ending with a crash,
as all leftist revolutions do.
He relies on me to keep
his sanity, he says,
knowing those words alone
will bring me closer to losing mine.
Guilt can be built
much quicker than a wall.

Labor

We planted white pine where a storm depression
had squatted on the flat glacial soil leaving trees horizontal.
Our rows were haphazard, born from the fatigue
of carrying water two pails at a time from a pump
almost half-a-mile away and the fact we couldn't tell
where the rows would end, some trick of scale
when one end is a shocked cornfield and the other
a swamp full of swale grass and only dead wood in between.
Fran, our supervisor, shoveled every hole
a seedling went in, tamped with one foot,
stood on the other like a stork,
spent all day on her feet,
complained that the storm should have left her
one truck to lean on, to sit back on, to sleep.
Fangs of pain bit into our backs,
concrete poured overnight to fix
our lumbar locked like wrought iron.
Three thousand pines later, she told us,
and you'll know what a woman feels after birth.

The Falling Man

The tower's gray and white stripes
like a corduroy curtain behind him,
the man, dark-skinned, wearing
a pale sports coat & black slacks,
the man isn't falling. I've superglued
the photo upside-down to the inside
of my closet door. He isn't falling,
one knee lifted, arms rigid, trapping
the billowing skirts of his jacket
against his sides. He's anyone
I can imagine. The father of many girls.
An expert on the language of Greenland,
which has no expletives. A novice stepdancer
practicing his routine. Sometimes, when
no one's around, I open the closet door
& say, "Good morning, Dancing Man."

R.T. CASTLEBERRY

The Eventual Silence

Wrapped around my father's neck
was a patriarch's gift—
a wire twined tight
these words hang upon.
He drank himself to the door
with half-steps and a South Georgia story.
His memory assigned death
to argument, to confession.
Aligned with decay,
he fed cigarettes to his asthma,
bourbon benders to his work routine.
Slumped in a sleeper's chair
there was no deity, no July,
no advice dispensed without death.
The difficult are easiest
to deal with as history.

R.T. CASTLEBERRY

To Thirst (Beneath the Sun)

Nearly November
the seasons read as unsettled,
wither into wariness.
Whether service, tithing
or strength of witness,
the right shape of redemption eludes me.
I wake to my resentments--
short rations, a silent phone,
the bristle of poverty's labor.
Staggering tired,
I take a sunrise turn,
cigarettes and cinnamon gum
to cover the morning drinks.
Hard hat workmen at
homestead building sites,
sleepy runaways in the homeless park
begin their rising rounds.
The newspaper I stole from a neighbor
smudges my hands with colored ink.
"A War Declared" is the headline.
"Details, B-16."

ALAN CATLIN

Marianne Moore at the Brooklyn Zoo 195–

standing by the animal cages
she is the Last Duchess of Brooklyn
dressed in high finery: a black cloak,
high, buttoned-at-the-neck- frilly blouse,
and her signature wide brimmed hat.

She is imperious,
inscrutable,
incorrigible
at the zoo:

a length of straw
in one hand,
a white rose in the other.

A zebra gnaws on
the heavy duty wire
behind her almost seems
to be mugging for the camera,
posing as a new incongruity
for a poet's mythic garden.

Moonstruck

She stopped dreaming
about the same time the roaches
started to talk in her ears.

Apocalyptic things—
their spindle legs. A thousand or more—
pops of a needle through canvas.

She hears the grind of antennae
the Styrofoam screech of folding
wings, the chatter—scattered
between the cracks
of her eyes.

Still, she listens
thin as an eyelash,
cigarettes in a line—
the embers of one ignite the next
under the pendulum moon.

She sleeps when they sleep.
Eyes faced inward, swallowing
the flaps and chirps
between her ears.

I set her coffee down and run for the bus.
It will all be cold by the time she wakes.

The palms

Her voice, when she spoke,
was a thousand years of the ocean rubbing
sharp things into sand.
She was there to play the lotto.
But she spoke to me about the palms,
bent into crosses and tied with ribbon.
They hung on a wall in her garage,
lay on her mother's grave at Easter.

She counted out her change in singles.
Again, to be sure
—Have you gotten your palms?—
        Of course I hadn't.
        I don't believe in those things.
        What does He know of a pillar in salt?

Her voice was a thousand years
of pine needles swept under the stairs.
She offered a blessing, I, a valediction.
Each of us held tight to our chances.
The palms, yellowed orphans
in the parking lot, ribbons bright
and stiff against the eastern breeze.

She rocked toward her empty garage.
I spit out the sea.

SHERRY CHANDLER

American History: Wayne

We tumbled up and down those oil-soaked stairs
like so many dung beetles rolling the Sisyphean ball
of burgeoning sexuality—in pairs
sometimes, holding hands in the halls—
most often in cliques, town or farm, and all
indifferent to the crumbling exoskeleton,
the shabby classrooms in a building already condemned.

I classed the boys by hairstyle, leaned toward crews,
or flat-tops, only eyed the pompadours
bunched behind the lunchroom, smoking. I'd choose
one year, Kenneth, so clean cut his forehead
was shiny, the next, Jimmy, tall, dark, and foreign,
a summer crush, and one time, for a lark,
I chased down Russell and kissed him on his Mohawk.

But in sixth grade, my heart settled on Wayne.
In token of fidelity we wore,
two jagged halves of one heart—on chains
around our necks for all to see—scored
with something sappy in rhyme. If there was more,
it's flushed from recall by the rush of years. We parted
I don't know why or when or who kept the heart.

Wayne became the farmer of his destiny,
prospered through hard work, the American myth
sold us in that falling-down school. Occasionally
his name dropped in conversation and I'd miss
him. At the forty-year reunion I'm told he
asked for me but I'm not one to reminisce.
He died before the fiftieth. Where the school
once stood there's a wasteland of weeds and rubble.

American History: James

(Setting Kentucky burley)

Uncle James steps like his legs
are stilts and every step he takes
he jobs the jobber in the ground

and my big sister throws a plant
like a dart down the tube.
Uncle James pulls the trigger,

the jobber's jaws clank open,
spit out the plant like the whale
spits out Jonah in my book.

Step
job
clank

Uncle James shouts "water boy." I go,
fast as I can. Dirt pulls at my feet.
Water splashes my legs. The bucket bail

cuts my palm. Sweat bees sting the bend
of my knees. I cry but Uncle James says
sweat bees only sting lazy people.

DAVID CHORLTON

A Day's Work

The workers next door have packed
up their tools and prepared
to go home. Early this morning
they began swinging picks
to break up the earth, then dug
narrow trenches for a system
to water the lawn, placed lengths
of pipe and tamped down the soil
to cover them while a tiny radio
played music from Mexico.
They didn't clock on or clock off,
but stayed for as long as it took
to finish the work of making rain
come out of the ground, which is
the kind of miracle it takes
for some men to stay alive.

DAVID CHORLTON

The Witness

The sunlight turns suddenly grey
when the first sign
appears to the south
of an approaching dust wall
that begins with a field
standing on edge
and moving toward us.

It has been a tranquil afternoon
for the mockingbirds
who pause from their springtime
aerobatics to sing
from the tops of power poles, and for
the lost dogs whose photographs
are posted beneath them
and who wander

all day and night. Now an eager wind
stirs in boughs
filled with yellow blossoms
and palm fronds claw the air
as it darkens. We brace ourselves,
close the windows,
and take aspirin

enough to hold off
a storm. What comes next?
A siren strikes up its note of madness
on McDowell Road. Visibility
closes in. The woman
who walks daily through
the neighborhood
offering to share
her biblical tracts with anyone

is wearing down her shoes
in panic, having checked
her watch and seen the time
she warns about
to be finally
at hand.

Outside Cheyenne

If not for the bones in the box
stall we would be in that house
on Quarter Circle Five, the wind
tearing down the Snowy Range
like a runaway truck on the wrong
side of Laramie. They were kittens
once, frozen together in the mud.
The realtor joked they'd make decent
wind chimes and we laughed.

We liked the view and the way the house
hunkered down in the vault of the hillside,
the wind screaming over the old tin roof
like a feral thing come home.

SARA CLANCY

When the test to predict Alzheimer's is available

I will be away from my desk
on a road trip to the Wind River Range. I will be drinking
coffee from a cardboard McDonald's cup. Or I will be home,
hanging Marianne's stained glass in the kitchen window or laundry
on a line. I will be kneading sour dough, writing poems or texting dog
pictures to my daughter. Straightening an oil painting of the three of us
in Manzanita, Oregon. Filling the hummingbird feeder. Reading an electronic
book published in 1813. Feeding my fish. Listening to *Ladies of the Canyon*.
I will be crocheting colors of my great grandmother into another new blanket.
Reminding my mother that she changed her password
and my father that I am his daughter
and my name is Sara.

Other Serpents

The garter snake says
that he has seen
the miracles of god
in the curve of the sea-
shell set down in dirt.

The red racer talks
of angels with mosquito
wings. The buzz
like a bell ringing
out backwards.

Even the rattler speaks
in tongues about
the way the sky
seen just right can look almost
the same as the sea.

Charles

Charles scrutinizes your ears,
Says, according to Zen, long lobes
Indicate intelligence. I shake my hair
To hide mine. He says a crooked
Little finger means deception,
Vertical frown lines divulge rage.

He has made a moss garden
With stepping stones and has not
Eaten flesh in 35 years. He is the winner
Of the forest preserve haiku contest.
His entry inscribed on his green cup.
They sold out too quickly so
We'll have to do without.

He's recently installed a woodstove
In his great room. It was cumbersome
To wrestle for a man his age. Skinny.
Grey ponytail. Bad teeth. His house
On the river needs repair. He'll die
In it. That reverse mortgage he took.

Last week in Whole Foods
He was suddenly faint. The cardiologist
Gave him pills, but what he intends to do
Is meditate and maybe get some solar panels.

JOAN COLBY

Charles in December

The arctic ice is melting and pretty soon.
Globally speaking, most of Florida's
Coast will be submerged. Charles
Is worried but optimistic.
Instinct will meld with intuition
Flowing to us from the future
And a spirit of cooperation
Is destined to bloom like a
Century plant. Charles' explanation
Of the tipping point involves
Nuclear fusion. His pale eyes
Penetrate the confusion that irritates
Lamar who says geologists
Have assured him that fracking
Has no negative consequence.
Charles says such illusions
Strip him of hope. Lamar
Thanks him for the philosophy
Lesson, gets his coat to head home
To his retirement acreage in The Windings,
Clumping on his new ceramic hip.
Charles folds his hands and sighs:
I'm just a guy living on a dead end
Above the river.

C. CLEO CREECH

Symmetry

It was not until
the slow steady swelling
the lump no longer ignorable
that I was reminded
the human need
for symmetry
unsettled by
something on this side
not on the other
something out of tune.
out of alignment, balance.

It was after
the surgeon's steady knife
the long crescent scar
that I was reminded again
the human need
for symmetry
something missing, gone
finger tips tracing
where something used to be.

Claire Brought Baseballs

We were told to bring
the usual things,
toiletries and sundries,
the common, the everyday,
items on well stocked shelves,
we take for granted.

Toothpaste and vitamins,
disposable razors, soap.
calcium pills and Tylenol,
refillable lighters,
old magazines and books—
but Claire brought baseballs.

Two big mesh drawstring bags
of beautiful perfect spheres,
with tight red stitching
and magic words like:
"Official" and "Major League"
two big bags of unhit home runs.

She would pitch one into the air,
the world would stop, stand still,
even clocks holding their breath.
then the flash of recognition,
the flailing arms and mad rush,
the clouds of shouts and dust.

There the crowd of youthful faces,
staring at this unexpected treasure,
this holy relic fallen from the sky.
History and heroes, hopes and dreams,
rolled up tight like the strings inside,
all suddenly made tangible and real.

Their shadow game played with sticks,
hitting wads of tight wound rags,
suddenly forgotten and cast aside.
for holding this cow-skin crystal ball
they could see the ballpark, swing of the bat
the uniforms, the cheering crowds.

And when I ever need to recall
the magic possible in children's eyes
the power of dreams and hope
even where hope is scarce
I remember that trip to Cuba
when Claire brought baseballs.

JIM DAVIS

On Virtue

Today I exchanged headphones for sounds of scraping
shovels. I pushed a guy out of his spot,
snowed in, two pit-bulls in the back seat
snouting through empty Cheetos bags. The Great

Beast of the city, as Simone Weil would say,
conjuring Plato, was quietly cracking
its knuckles above us, blizzarding diminutive
callous. The city sighs, forgetting the end

of winter is near. Lawn chairs claim cleared
spots with signs that say, *Mine—I plowed,
I park, and Truth is the summit of the known.* We
know who is kind by the gravity of his character.

Did Emerson say what's at the center of the act
is loving oneself? Aphorism in the water
of anaphora—sound of my scraping shovel, sound
of vanilla virtue, sound of the sound of the Great

Beast shredding lampshades into ceremonies, escape
plans manufactured in the basement of a textile plant.
I am everything at once and I travel by imagi
nation, can you hear me? If so my weight's decided.

So and so made a career painting *Poetry
is Dead* on coffee cups. So and so
painted all that concerned his better nature.
Nature consumed the body of a boy at the bottom

of a river. It's best to assume the way things are
is better than the story that begins with a princess
lost in the fig trees. I've lost my hands, he said,
I have winter eyes. Standing still

amid the silent snow is our best impression
of dying. When we were young we'd do anything
not to be the ones who raised us, misunderstanding
virtue. Misunderstanding how what's expected

denies our best impression. Finish what you started,
my father said, referring to everything. Character
begins where the shovel enters, truth in the minor
blizzards I create along the driveway. Falling
exhalations, *I strive to comprehend thee.*
The Great Beast shovels everything.

JIM DAVIS

Bell Cow

Where I go is of little consequence.
Thousands more like me. Walt rode the trolley

with a paper sack of peaches on his lap.
Someone turned up the radio in the bread shop.

Someone tuned the radio to prophecy.
My body is nimble. Certainty's not probable.

You are the barnyard, no you are the barnyard—
Yes I said, I know I said, talking to myself again.

Bread goes hard then soft in a paper sack.
The barn is a bowl of lemons. Subtle rafters.

Yes, I loved you then, in the unselfish summer
before the river was a river made of crows.

The auction of our better selves, carving
limestone totems. Fruit fly pressed into

the reflection of a crows over the shoulder
of a boy reflecting bits of the city he remembers.

The trolley jumped track and settled in a garden.
It was red. It was blue. Bell cow roiled in the hay.

MICHAEL DIEBERT

Marriage

The memory hits him like seawater
to the face, and he shudders:

years ago, stuck in a different persona,
driving the hatchback

down some nondescript county road,
passing tobacco barns, sensing

there was not and never would be
a house or a woman to keep him around,

total control, therefore no point
in feeling anything but good.

He exits the interstate,
sees three saplings

planted in the median, green limbs
straining toward the sun, bees

murmuring and drunk on their mission.
It takes his breath. So much so

he pulls into the church parking lot
to wait it out.

A long time he lived by himself.
These days, he and his wife

go to lots of celebrations
with lots of food and familiarity,

and he often sits off to the side
oohing and aahing,

sometimes just nodding,
and he's grateful and perfectly content

to be ensconced, to have time
both behind and in front of him.

He recites this under his breath.
When newlyweds burst from the sanctuary

and run through a shower of birdseed,
he rolls down his window

and provides the loudest cheer of all.
Then, another feeling

and another vision, a strange one:
a man in a leather jacket,

motorcycle helmet under his arm,
sunglasses in place of eyes,

stubbled chin, stubborn jaw, standing
in the middle of pink and red

azaleas—rooted to the spot,
bending toward the light—

not quite himself, not quite not.

DONNARKEVIC

Needle on Vinyl

In her bedroom, my sister plays
the latest 45's, *Love Me Do,*
My Guy, A World Without Love...

She has no guy and no love,
only the crackles, blips,
and scratches that exist

when the needle circles the vinyl
around words like *true, heartbreak,*
happy, loneliness, moon...

From her window she stares
at the round white scar in the sky,
a pool where the tears of stars collect,

a place void of sound or harmony,
breathless, a remote loveless disc
with no B-side.

DONNARKEVIC

On Never Leaving West Virginia

The slope mines I work never cross state lines.
I am clothes-torn naked-dirty; I am the seam.
New hand-me-down overalls, the creases stiff
as a dead man's fingers. My Uncle Aubrey's
death scared me, never touched a corpse,
died in his sleep, Aunt May waking up,
knowing before she turned over just from the cold,
like when the coal furnace dies.

Carried the pall, watched the gravediggers
crank the coffin into the earth without a glitch.
Sometimes I hear the sound in nightmares,
the roof of the mine giving way,
the company weighing options:
The vein's petered out,
only one man, a fossil now.
What's the use? At twenty-two,
it ain't like he's goin' nowhares.

WILLIAM DORESKI

Collapse of the Austro-Hungarian Empire

Up too early in the frost
I allow my heart to wring itself
like a sorry scrap of laundry.
Your indifference has rebuked me

so thoroughly the starless sky
looks flimsy as the plastic lid
of a trash can. Today you'll pose
in various public places

with whatever grace or awkwardness
suits you. Slurping herbal tea
or pawing through the library
with a fistful of index cards

you'll make no effort to look
as luscious as a vampire
but will achieve a great distance
no simple argument can span.

I've appetite enough to sustain
both of us against a hunger
as vast as the Caspian Sea.
But you don't want to believe me

when I step away from my psyche
and critically assess its mass.
You don't want to accept the gray
I flaunt at the end of a stick,

don't believe it's a human relic
remaindered after hundreds of lives.
Enjoy your tea, enjoy researching
the collapse of the Austro-

Hungarian Empire. The dark
bleeds its invisible colors,
decorating the sacred parts
of your body against your will.

ROBERT EASTWOOD

Resurrection

Besides making love you need to walk,
said the doctor, so I sauntered in the park
to forget my heart. Ahead, under sycamores,

in lacewing leaf-shade, she palmed her hair
like a teen reveling at the touch of it. Perhaps a bee
she'd flicked away? She dropped her brush

into a nomad market cart heaped with plastic bags.
When she turned—a ruddiness, a painted grin,
more gum than teeth—I saw one hand held scissors,

the other, a newspaper page. She laid them
in the cart, no, on the black mesa of a bag.
A ritual began, sequencing invisible things,

waving a pencil, placing strings.
I felt the velvet-eared succulence of sun
as it threaded the sycamores. Breezes shirred

the leaves—everywhere, a spate of dapples.
"Spare some change, mister?" With an index
drilling her cheek, she bent her knee,

one varicosed leg out-stretched to curtsy.
Lacing the cart's basket-wires, paper dolls
with crayoned faces, each a unique posture.

Scarves of light danced on her theater
of tissue bodies. The bags bubbled like tar
in the agitated, irresolute sun.

For a buck she offered me a paper doll
made of newsprint, this odd woman,
who pulsed in a sun-tapestry. I walked on

with a body, a face, without smudge.
A chest, committed to my palm, throbbed
at the wobble of my thumb.

The sun-pitched, shuddering leaves, the whole
mysterious way into which I walked,
thrummed in the splendor of my heartbeat.

How to Live to Die in Vegas

Maybe it's the ropey vein on her temple
thumping a tempo of military zeal that says it all,
that says, fuck off, I'm winning, buster.
    Maybe it's the grin she wears like an old Buick.

Maybe the angry, devil-be-damned intent.
What about this woman, what about this place,
about this mecca of Tea Party piques,
    desert replicas of the Forum & Sphinx?

It isn't her oat-bucket handbag, her floral
moo-moo, nor the oxygen bottle she's wheeled in
coupled to a pulsing, viscid tube,
    dangling above her heart.

Nor her Camel butts smoldering
like a spent auto-da-fé.
Everyone smokes connected to some threat
    they've wheeled to Vegas.

She keeps jabbing the buttons, her yam-like
fingers have the intransigence of certainty.
She sits in a cornucopia of trills & bells,
    marches, booms & toots unceasing—

the Kodacolor screen spinning
bananas & cherries, jokers & chevrons.
She ignores the washboard-thresh of banjos
    from the gazebo above the bar.

Let her be. Let her be amid the jack-
hammer din, for this is Las Vegas:
cavalier with ruin, dismissive of nuance.
    Let her feed the electric maws

that are virgin to a knurled coin
but hum a tally on LEDs under a smoky nimbus,
impersonal as drones—
    let her go until the game plays out

    or she explodes, for it's all a show
ablaze in neon anyway, & shows must end.
It's a trailer length away from heaven,
    the draw of greed, the revenge of Indians.

RICHARD FEIN

Beyond Where I Was Allowed to Go

Rode my bike a bit beyond where I was allowed to go.
Saw a small man on the ground
helpless under the shadow of a hefty woman.
She was a storm cloud hurling lightning at him.
Tears and blood rained from his face.
Then she saw me,
and I rode quickly away back to the grocery store
which marked the border of my childhood world.
When safely within I dared a second look.
Scariest was her face,
no longer angry it seemed featureless,
a blank circle, a half-drawn stick figure.
His face was forgettable even before I saw it.
The next day I again biked past the grocery store
and went farther, even farther till it was out of sight,
for there were so many scary things I had to see
beyond where I was allowed to go.

The Genesis of Human Family Dysfunction

Contemplate those ridiculous fig leaves on Adam and Eve.
Why the sudden shame, for after some time together
a husband and wife will surely yawn at each other's nakedness.
Or imagine mismatched newlyweds the morning after a Las Vegas quickie wedding,
lying hungover and nude in bed with the hotel shades open
and the sun glaring into their half-sober eyes,
realizing that last night's dice roll came up snake eyes
and the slot machines served only a hodgepodge of sour fruit
as all cash needed for a quickie divorce was devoured
in the coin slots of bad risks.

RICHARD FEIN

Freedom Rules

I was afraid that the bee would knock herself out.
Over and over it butted the window glass
trying to reach freedom among the flowers outside.
And the teacher droned on about stability;
how atoms trade electrons to complete their outermost shells,
two electrons in the first, then eight, then eighteen....
"Why not three or seven or eighteen and a half," I asked.
"It's the rule," he said, "it's the rule.
Without rules there's no molecular glue
to bind the universe together."
I watched the bee flit nearer and nearer
to that smallest gap between glass and frame.
But the teacher growled,
"Pay attention, eyes front, stop asking stupid questions,
and memorize the rules that govern stability."
My eyes snapped front,
for it was his classroom, his universe, and his rules,
so I never saw the bee fly free
through the opening to the flowers outside.
And right now I am writing this,
pursuant to standard grammatical rules
as I misunderstand them.

The Hi-Tech Sabbatical

Last night you dreamed a dream.
You were out in the dinghy
scudding the bottom again
and a great fish lifted you out
of the water and the long wake
of a tanker rolled you over.

As the sea took you down
and in spite of your panic
your limbs kept crossing
and recrossing themselves
as though to bless the world
if not your own outfit
for giving its key personnel
time off to rebrood themselves
for the hi-tech world
of greater Seattle.

Later, you bobbed off rocks
among spaghetti plants
and animals with comic eyes,
a bed of eels, absolute cold.

When the crabs assembled
you saw their claws waving
endlessly like wands as though
you were part of some magic
they would like to perform.

WILLIAM FORD

Smart Phone Blues

Baby, ever since we split,
two kinds of music play
inside my head,
a Billie Holiday in the dress
of every woman's blues
and a *Kindertötenleider,*
Mahler's dead hug
for the child in himself.

They're about us, of course,
you, singing true soul
perched by some piano
while I finger bass
in another dive, both
hip to Apps and Skype,
ready to Talk and Text,
ready to forgive.

Midnight Mass

Familiar hymns scratch the dust
attempting to release angels.
They gather in the candlelight,
weep for these husks of men,
their skeletal dance, bone against bone,
where nobody remembers the steps.

The soft melody returns
against the percussion of rosaries.
It follows us through the pews
on the bitter smell of incense.

It is the way the Host is a hot coal
held against the tongue
to light the path for prayer,
the way our breaths become
a caravan of pilgrims desperate
for a taste of thunder.

We'd like to return to a place
of myth or tumescent ardor
but this is the hour of rain
and shuddering wind. We step
from the narthex to the sobriety
of twilight, and even the angels
rub their wings together to make fire.

Choosing Bowls

I pour cereal in a little bowl,
she a big one. I chide her

for wasting, using more
than needed, try to make

her smaller than world
she hopes to fill.

Clink of spoon on ceramic.
Taste of regret.

Next morning at breakfast
she opens cupboards quietly,

pours cereal in two
big bowls, hands me one.

JAMES GRABILL

Being Suspended Within Being

We can't know longing in the world that led to our birth or damages done by the gods, only what the place has become.

Where night rolls out in its ten-ton trucks, consciousness is one tree in the forest we'd want to avoid clear-cutting.

At some point, single-celled beings reached into fin-making for their star-needled tidal swims. Isn't each second, hour, or millennium an exotic process of regeneration?

As honey-hive prairies carry on in back of gray-whale Pacific rains, a freezing hot whole range of slightest shifts falls in and out of sync.

If old-world heaviness frames the moment between opposing ends, isn't this a chance, if only a moment, to hear and be heard?

Where the mind is, however the place looks now, classical circulation feeds muscle memory and spontaneity. Disciplines convene in the smallest spectroscopic spike, as the rake of the spectrum returns to sea.

The warp of winds breaks up into fractal spin, gamma ray telescopes registering the Big Bang echo.

The way Earth looks from space, a place interconnected, smaller than ancestors thought, what happens next could suddenly appear.

Branches Shaken by Light

It's raining and cold in this part of the spectrum. The tree in the spine holds up, but what are we doing with our birds?

The past fills with emphasis, and empties each second before moving ahead. Arboreal rhizome makes core-spun seedlings sound. What happens next takes on necessity, as light reverberates within the spectrum.

A branch of the genome carries the shuck of mammoth breath.

Fallen leaves blow through layers of mushroom soils.

Overhead miles have their stretches of wing flying in further world.

Doesn't being here live in its forest? Doesn't the hour lengthen and shorten, depending on moss-green powers of ten?

A hundred-foot blue whale might draw up in a swell a few thousand lives from human thought. Breath fills lungs and overflows, guiding the Beethoven quartet in fluid time.

The warp of winds breaks into fractal spin where the moment's taken on weight, transporting parts of the future into the present.

A light of raw solar ore transplants energy in leaves and falls through Gauguin paintings into circulation of cells.

The future flies over on the shoulder of water. The compass eye aligns within cells, where a small cusp reflects the whole.

Green Chain

The three parallel chains clank
as they bring green lumber
out of the mill
to where the graders
slash their marks
with thick blue crayon

and then on to me
where I grab the boards with
soggy gloved hands
and stack them

I work an eight-hour shift
but because there's alcoholism
in the world
and irresponsibility
I sometimes work a double
I've worked as much as a triple
24 hours straight

I'm strong
my mind goes numb
my mind is no more complex than a moth's
the crew chief likes my work ethic
the fog rolls in and out

Immigration officers scream in
In my brain-dead state I think they're taxi drivers
the amber light makes the white cars yellow
I just keep pulling lumber
I'm legal
My papers are in order

My name is Gonzalez
but it might as well be Johnson

A coworker told me that Johnson
is the most common American name
I thought it might be Smith
or Jones
but this guy said he knows
because his name is Johnson

I told him Gonzalez is a common
name in Mexico
but I don't know
where it sits on the Hit Parade

Johnson smiled at that one
Johnson is missing a lot of teeth
They have rotted out of his head

Being Wrong

It is a practice.
I notice how difficult it is
to be wrong and loving
as if being wrong were some great fault
carried against me
the hand of a friend clenched in anger
a harsh word spoken by my mother
the car behind me starting too early at a stoplight
slamming against mine, sending my head bouncing
on the thin armature of my neck.

So I must rest
with my own wish
to push my wrong away from me.
Sit,
cross legged,
the bowl of my body open,
hands on knees,
my heart an offering,
my wrongness a light
I shine from its center.

Fishing Prohibited from Bridge

For a flash of fin, or the white-bellied
carpet-flap of a big stingray,
I spent the best times of my youth
(one week a year) standing
on the scalding concrete of south
Florida, staring down into the roil
of coffee-colored tidal rivers,
as if my puny line could pull up answers
to all those angry currents of home
that always drug us kids toward
their undertow.
We felt fangs, razor shells, and eely
insinuations, stood stings and shocks
whose reasons stayed hidden from us,
and probably always will,
though that doesn't stop me now
from dragging my hangovers out of bed
at dawn and driving through palms
and reddening mornings to yet
another, hoping maybe someday it
will be the one to carry me over
the old doubts of dark water.

Requiem

Sanibel Island, Florida

She came down the beach, oddly
overdressed in the heat, walked
past me, sitting
in the dunes.
When she stopped,
she looked both ways
to make sure no one
was looking,
took off her backpack,
set it down in the sand,
rolled up her jeans, took
something out, waded
into the surf
and emptied the urn,
the cloud rising above her head
taken by the breeze out to sea.

I walked out to meet her
when she was done:
"May I ask who that was"?

She was trembling so bad,
she could hardly speak:
"My husband."

I said, "It's because
I've asked my wife
to do that for me."

Then, "He loved this island."
"Me too," I said.

As she made her way back down the shore,
the ibises, gulls, and pipers
parted for her,
and then, later,
for me.

PAT HANAHOE-DOSCH

Taps

1.

Every night he falls into sleep
      to "Taps" played over loudspeakers
           on wooden poles. Every night, the sound
of a trumpet or bugle playing that song.
      Every night, in the space
           between awake and dying
dream: his sister's coffin perched above its grave,
      waiting to be lowered into it,
           green felt draping the edges,
white carnations scattered along the lid like rain.
      Stabbed to death by her ex-husband.

2.

Every night, he unfurls
      into his sleeping bag into
           the same song the Army plays
every night
      and at funerals to honor the dead.
           Then he wakes into an Afghan morning, silent and dark.
The base wakes into every morning
      to sand brushing against tent walls,
           to the heat, like a crematorium.

3.

Except some days they are missing someone.   Or another.
      Some days tap along in the dust,
           some days don't. Some days
are for explosions and shrapnel and bits of shredded skin.
      Some days tap into night with just enough
           rain so poppies can grow, red stains
blossoming
      in rivulets across the mountains
           where the women are masked in blue drapes
or buried in mud walls.

PAT HANAHOE-DOSCH

Orectic

1.

The swallows skirr in formation
toward a distant copse of trees.
Somewhere, the scarecrow and tin man

are still winding their way through Oz
with no heart, no brain, no Dorothy, no witches,
and only the magic they can make on their own.

Tornadoes are the summer's vengeance on insurance companies,
and the local houses are sealed to the ground
tightly by concrete and asphalt.

Still, some little girls love to dance in red shoes,
will even glue on red glitter to make them sparkle
as they skirr around the yard, pretending

to flee from flying monkeys, though, really,
those black wings are just a goshawk hunting
for something much smaller and crunchier.

2.

The children's screams and shouts,
laughter and splashing from a plastic pool
drift up and down the streets, invade

the open windows of the neighbors who think
of vanilla birthday cake with butter cream and coconut
icing with lemon filling, or chocolate brownies
sprinkled with walnuts, and mounds of pistachio ice cream.

Actually, the children are being served a simple
sheet cake from Costco with an icing drawing
of pirates waving from a ship spread over the yellow confection.

The birthday girl blows out the seven candles and wishes
that her dad would stay there and not go home

to his other wife, and her mother wishes
she didn't have to see that same man again, ever,
and the father is sorry he came,
and the other children all want to break
the piñata and eat the candy before anything else.

The mothers force dusty, hot smiles as they serve hot dogs.
No one knows about the chemicals in the water
and in the ground these houses were so quickly built on,

though in ten years they will wish they had known, had never lived
in that small circle in the city built by a company that was bought up
in a hostile takeover about five years after that party.
Lawsuits will be futile. The Emerald City protects its emeralds.

3.

The body in the coffin looks like
a muppet that has been thrown away.
Empty of the hands that gave it substance,
it lies, flattened and colorless against the white pillow and lining of the box.

The girl's mother can't breathe enough air,
her chest feels as though someone is trying to split her
breast bone with a hammer and large nail,
her stomach is full of mosquitos and horse flies, biting, biting,
and her mouth is cracked wood, like the railing of the deck
over the back yard behind her house.

The girl's classmates gather together to one side
of the funeral parlor room. Movies and TV shows
haven't prepared them for this. Their adolescent awkwardness
trumps the grief they don't quite know how to feel yet.

They will know its muddy flood when they wake up tomorrow
and she's not there to play a video game, or at band practice,
when there is no clarinet playing slightly out of tempo to tease,
and no one to cheat off of in algebra, anymore.

Now they just wonder why she looks like that,
and what they should say to her mother. They are counting
on their own mothers to do that for them,

but their fathers nudge them over to the receiving line
and they have to hug her, they have to tell her
they will miss the girl too. And they mean it.

They don't know she will be only a distant memory in a few years.
Two of them will join her, though buried in different cemeteries.
The others will move away. The houses will sell at a loss.
One father will declare bankruptcy, another, take a lower salary
two states away, and all will lose touch with everyone.

There is nothing, really,
they can say to each other, anyway.
The borders of Oz are impassable.

Chrome

I'd like to be
that bit of sun
racing between
reciprocating trees
to sluice your eye from
the grade of the road

Slip-sliding between
the evergreen blinds
on a late afternoon drive,
the moon but a glimmer
in the pink of
your mirror

With knuckles curled
around ten and two
and Rickenbackers chiming
a well-traveled tune,
as you squeeze
some more lead
from the end
of your day

Just a bit of chrome
to bounce off
the shield.

Lascaux

I have never seen anything
more pregnant of Man
than the riderless horses
etched in black
on the warm-blooded wall
of a cave in France

Staggered by design
and baptized in time,
one's mouth pried open
as if to say:

You are a knot
in the line,
my flickering friend,
a torch's wick,
the scattered scent,
an apocalypse of hooves
passing over the bridge

Whose echo
is written
in the silence
we grip

Bernoulli's Equation

the difference in pressure
between your heart
and your head
as you're about to cry
and trying desperately not to

cannot be solved
by Bernoulli's equation

no matter the wry
point of pride you might feel
in recovering this scrap
of classroom junk,
so fleeting because

you can't recall
the equation's specifics

or the first thing about its
application and uses

which seems fitting
in your present state,
as you can't rationalize
the plug in your throat
or quite find the air
to explain yourself

except that it's something to do
with the difference between

what you are
and
what you thought

yourself to be

and how that can shift
in the blink of an eye

KATHERINE HOERTH

For Those Who Search the Peak of Ararat

It hurts to hope so hard, to search the peak
of Ararat, knees to the icy ground.
They must have heard, as we have, how the earth's
too old for such a flood, and that an ark

this vast could not be born from just two pairs
of hands, a simple man, his nameless wife.
But men still comb the endless hills of hope
for planks of ancient wood beneath the snow

with perfect carbon date, the bones of beasts
that Noah may have rescued from the flood,
an olive branch's imprint etched in stone.
Like us, they come home empty armed. *We'll try*

again next month, you say. I force a smile.
We'll climb into the snowy sheets and search
our bodies' peaks for miracles beneath
the surfaces of silk, of skin, of flesh.

KAREN PAUL HOLMES

My Almost Date With a Cowboy, Polebridge, Montana

Maybe an ex-pro-hockey player, now cattle broker doesn't qualify as a cowboy.
And him trailing my girlfriend, her husband, and me from the Bandit Saloon
to the Northern Lights Bar at their country club isn't what you'd call a date.
So I guess I should call it my almost date with an almost cowboy, though he did
have on needle-toed cowboy boots. He'd been watching football while apparently
throwing back beer or maybe shots all day, wore a Montana Grizzlies sweatshirt
and wasn't that cute. When he ordered a Jägerbomb so loud everyone in the
fireplaced lounge could hear, we felt like crawling under the table. Plus my friends
had briefly considered setting me up with him but thought better because he always
had at least two women strung along, one in Canada and one or possibly two here.
All that said, he was the first man to flirt with this newly single woman who hadn't
dated since 1977. Him being so drunk he would not remember slurring once every
three minutes, "You're hot!" and "You're leaving tomorrow?" shouldn't have flattered me.
But it did.

Diamond, Post Divorce

sits in the black vault
so sure of its white brilliance
snug on its circle of platinum
awaiting another finger
forever.

KAREN PAUL HOLMES

Poem that Begins with a Definition

A passive sentence is often composed by a passive
person. It is written with a subject acted upon
by a verb, sort of like being assaulted.
A phantom subject is preferred by governments,

corporations and scientists: *Written complaints*
will be read and answered in three days.
It has been decided you are not eligible for benefits.
The solution was heated to boiling.

This idea was thought up by someone anonymous.
The similes were excavated one by one,
like grapefruit triangles with a serrated spoon.
Then, edits were marked by a red pencil.

This poem will be appreciated by people
who don't like action or responsibility.
This poem will be satisfying to few
because its conclusion was eaten by the dog.

In Praise of Poor Excuses

Blessed are the poor excuses
for they are inherently of earth.
Earth, that poor excuse for heaven.
Heaven, that worst excuse of all
for not showing up for your own
life here on earth, where all the poor excuses
live. Just listen to the poor excuses
singing together, hoisting another
draft of a poor excuse up to their lips
and spilling it down their shirtfronts,
and laughing the loudest, and telling the biggest
whoppers. And what on earth
are we to make of all the poor excuses
that we make here on earth? I say:
praise them. For they are in the world
and of it. For they are falling from the lips
like so many colorful, pathetic, beautiful
dead leaves dancing down and no one
is using them for anything except
maybe the children, and here and there
a few suspicious-looking grown-ups
gathering them into piles, into poems,
and digging around in them till evening comes,
and heading home with one or two
still sticking to their heads.

Lloyd

I had a friend named Lloyd when I was eight.
I will always remember Lloyd for his two l's
which came at the beginning. I didn't know
much. But I knew two l's could come at the beginning
already at the tender age of eight. Life went
on. I learned about llamas. And Prince Llewellyn.
And the Iliad, which doesn't have two l's
at the beginning, though it kind of looks like it does.
And eventually I lost touch with Lloyd although
I never forgot him. Because every single unlikely
superfluous thing, every odd doubling, or identical
twin at the beginning of anything, reminds me of Lloyd
and his two l's: the first one loud, capital, rushing
in; the second one silent, reticent, redundant as Lloyd himself.

A. J. HUFFMAN

Venus

The only flower in this desert is a cannibal.
Rooted and dying
of thirst, it still blooms. Scenting
its last breath to the wind. A buzzing
response. Hope is as simple as seeing
the next fly to trap.

A. J. HUFFMAN

Floating

In a delirium of pre-dawn stasis,
I have become a desert
of stars. Wandering the cosmos
in an insomniac haze, I have collected
these allegedly five-pointed passengers
along the way. To say they have been
misrepresented is an understatement. Not at all
finite or sharp, they burn ephemerally
tucked into my hair and the folds of my robe.
They have consumed me with their welcome
embrace, unjudgingly adorned me,
marked me as queen of exponential possibility.
Together we dance, wingless angels, hiding
from the sun.

Dockhands

You always said we should buy
an old yacht and fix her up,
and charter summers for the stars.
Then I'd pop some beers,
rub the pup's ears,
turn on the hose
and scrub—

salt, oil, seagull crap,
the sticky gunk from coolers.
Rotting planks replaced,
line around a cleat, *Watch your step,*
blistering heat and a two-buck tip,
Thank you, sir,

under buggy dock lights
pumping someone's shit.
Tow, recharge, provision. Another call
for fuel and ice.
The women say *He's nice,*
our old dog snoring.

HENRY HUGHES

On Sunday

On Sunday I zinc moss
hunching the shingles,
re-flash rain
into the right gutter,
straighten and screw down
the storm-whacked weather vane,

then wash my hands and sit down
for a juicy roast lamb
and a sunny talk
with my wife and two sons.

My youngest mentions the bats
hanging in the attic,
like *Spoiled monsters,* and we laugh.
The older boy tells us *They eat mosquitoes*
and are good for the environment,
and we nod.
My wife chews quietly, wipes her mouth,
then says, *They don't belong*
in this house. We look down at our
food for inspiration.

Squishing through blue guano,
I smell the cost of devotion,
and without a prayer
gas the bats into leaf bags.
The fallen weight of darkness
sagging in the street.

JOSEPH HUTCHISON

A Conflict Photo...

framed so tight we can't
tell if that fat fly's poised

on a moist rose petal or
the half-closed eye

of yet another child
(the same child always)

killed in whoever's
latest just war.

M. J. IUPPA

Frayed Dreams

When sleep's ragged breath ransacks our bedroom
and I wake to rumpled clothing left scattered on

the moonlit floor, I worry about my life here & how
my children's lives elsewhere may be suffering

the same hurried feats that can't be executed
with forethought, but seemingly fit into the scheme

of running late. A wild thought that makes me
think I have forgotten all the things that are working—

refrigerator, clock, the lonely faucet drip—sounds
that fill up one hour into the next, without recognition,

without any fuss, like that red star pulsing on a distant radio
tower knows, sooner or later, I'll look up & start listening.

MIKE JAMES

Discount Personal Mythology

for Bill Knott

when the gods visit to borrow
my soul for the night

i hope they don't enter through
the front door keyhole

no, let them fly in through
my bedroom window

it's normally half open
for wind and stars

i only ask when they leave
good dreams stay with me

let me visit some old friends
let me forget they are lost

CAROLE JOHNSTON

Aubade For My Father

you rise in sepia
like sun through empty trees
sycamore ghost

gold words scroll across your aura
I hear them through the camera of your eyes
leather and roses—stained glass and ink

poet who never read poetry
who taught me how to see
the vanishing luminous muse

I echo you back from
borders of namelessness singing
your name in my sleep

when you return
trailing mists of morning
I will know that you are still
a watcher of the dawn

LAURA M. KAMINSKI

Give Us a Moment Yet, Hesperides

for Jose and Andrea

Stay the legend
of that Greek garden
with its golden
apples and
its serpent-dragon—

don't bring it
over into Eden yet—
from where I sit
at the edge of both
the pasture

and November,
already this morning
I have counted
fifty-seven
things I don't

have names for. Adam,
I walked toward
the apple-tree
this morning, gave
into temptation

of a wider
horizon, and I've
fallen. And sitting
here in this damp
patch of grass,

I find despite
my fall I'm

unashamed, and we
are still in Eden
and we haven't

finished Naming
yet, not nearly.

LAURA M. KAMINSKI

Conversion

The trees are glass, lead crystal, woods by Waterford,
each limb, each trunk encased in ice, all their bark glazed smooth—
they creak beneath a Spanish moss of icicles.

The old elm, lopsided, frozen, overbalances,
with a slow groan lifts roots from the dark earth, leaving
them exposed, a naked ghost detached, its shell expired.

Gunmetal clouds swing open and the world shocks
with light, full-spectrum white hits the ice and splinters,
blinding, into rainbows—

I have seen the gates of heaven receive a fallen tree.

Everything returns to gray and blue and beige.
I remove my gloves and splay my twigs of fingers in the snow.
I want to change my name, change my tribe and my religion—

I want to join them—stand with them branch to branch
and never have to close my eyes.

The Woman With Glass In Her Face

Earthquake, 1974

She first appears in a cut crowd scene,
blue blouse, mustard bow,
handsome and middle-aged.

It's not until the earthquake is almost over
that we see her again, dodging a collapsing building,
a teenage daughter trailing behind her,
stumbling through the debris.
The girl calls out for her mom
and the woman turns her back to the camera.

That's when it happens.

From above, the sound of breaking glass,
then a guttural cry. She turns, face bloodied,
the shard embedded in her forehead.

It's almost believable; the way she staggers,
the way raspy *oh gods* spurt from her lips.
Today, the glass would have decapitated her,
head bouncing on the pavement like a basketball,
blood geysering from her neck like a Vegas fountain.

But this is 1974 and a mother impaled by glass
is about as much horror as we can stand.
The desensitization will begin in the 80s,
the viscera on the visor generation.
As LA breaks apart, this woman is giving us
30 seconds of raw, pure emotion before she falls
out of frame never to be seen again.

Who were you, lady?
Did anything come before or after?

Did you even get to meet Heston or Gardner?
Did you die on the sidewalk or were you taken
to the makeshift hospital in the car park
only to die in the flood and aftershock?
You should have been the star, the survivor,
the shard a trophy beaming from your exposed skull.

Edgar Brackle

My boys carry me to the river
and whisper my baptism like old men
finally wanting God. The sunrise
makes the willows forget the winter shore,
how it props me with my sons for a silence,
and gives me the same faith. I hear
their first words from long ago beginning
against time. I even hear some lost hounds
yowling before my own father lived.

I see my mother and grandmother fighting
before my birth. The December of their words
is swollen into my room. A few wrens
slant their voices across an island somewhere.
I have ridden a boat there many summers,
but I cannot hear them. The boys swim
then rebuild the gazebo and dock, and burn
some rotten boards on our beach. I'm home
with their minds again. The lopsided door
reveals a sunken field where Saponi kids
raced against a wildfire, their bodies taken
into the smoke like a dry sedge. I turn a key,
it is my own voice lingering with the door.

CLYDE KESSLER

Executions

We sang with dogs, cats, fools and ghosts
down a crooked road. And we watched lightning
steal a prisoner's sunrise. Whatever he knew
made his last day starve. What the wife kept secret,
the rain crows hollered across the tallest trees in Virginia
and nobody believed, just poured the mean bootleg,
kicked the long fence, waved cardboard protest signs
and then sat on the hill like dead birds hanging.

The story fit the clogged road. Some old women
hassled the judge's first born, made the law stand
cruelest by the mall. We sang to the saw-briers
and the swamp canes. Somebody with a preachy soul
swerved into the crowd, bloodied one of the women,
then ran. Lightning cracked an old pine on the hill.
Then we just watched the crooked road turn dark
towards a hole in the sky. Then we shut up.
Then we drove home.

CLYDE KESSLER

All the Mothmen

The dark wings know their heaven
is slowest where the red lilies stare.
It deepens a rainbow's mind into a cloud.

Some of the earth is scaled into their eyes,
and almost holds them awake with children
who have forgotten them, or left a door
wide open among the ghosts and old parents
who have no houses, or who leave no voice
like a mockingbird whickering to the sun
nearest a deaf woman.

I'm stationed there.
I pull your name from a hat at midnight.
The force of a name scribbled into a fire
has taken my hands. There's a nervous ink
written as a symbolic laugh, a narrow gate
is kicked from the fields. A wild dog
is digging after a lost creature with the summer
placed just like a skull under a stump.
It has a secret life timed to where they fly.

CLYDE KESSLER

Lies of the Poem

Birds are flying up from the bones
of their ancestors, such fool flightless things
wrapped with ashes from the earth's core.
Now you watch their wings hurry through clouds
to all their hungry babies that make no sense
with their wings already raised blind at each other.

It might always be a tall tale for talking lizards.
It might never bother you while you sample Jupiter in a lens.
The air soon fails. Fire gushes from inside a hidden voice.
Giant worlds explode. Earthy planets slide madly towards their stars.
Watery planets begin boiling or freezing nearly alive, or the atmospheres
thin into craters. Your spectrographs witness a lost cause, radio static
surrounds you. How you wish you could fly.

Creature

By darkness, I raise the stars.
I grieve my father beyond my words.
Sorghum withers, catbirds chortle
to a copperhead. It makes a sky begin
summering against the ground.

I'm a half-note frisked from Aldebaran.
Heat is singing its dust cloud to my roof.
My mother lowers a window and sweats
like a shadow, then drinks it from my mind.
A kitten climbs a chimney towards a ghost.

By darkness, I feed this midnight
some hungry shards of glass, trinkets
greened beyond my eyes like a war
I never dodge. If it fights me, I'm
home. If it embraces, I'm also home.

quiet clocks

Old photos in another language,
the people look vaguely the same.
Separated at birth, families cling
to umbilical cords of memory, powdered
thought collects in luggage stored
in rooms. Nothing is kept safe.

JENNIFER LAGIER

Grandpa's Hands

I remember his fists, hard knuckles
clipping a loudmouthed trespasser's chin.
At Basin Creek, he pulled a knife blade
through bellies of brook trout.

When I was thirteen, he braced
a twenty gauge shotgun against my shoulder,
placed his trigger finger over mine.
We ground-sluiced a dimwitted
mud hen together.

Later, after a series of strokes,
at the home where our family stored him,
he would wait for his grandchildren's
after-school visits, grin, silently reach
for our hands like a curious infant.

JENNIFER LAGIER

From Mother to Daughter

Life, you once said, is like cutting an onion:
you cry your way through it.

Tears rise like oven burns,
cover your forearms.

I think of you, slice what could
have been into family suppers.

Remember the drawer of stale
bread heels you used to curb hunger.

In dreams, your ghost weeps,
pries my mouth open.

Oracle

Spread-eagled
in the Venice Blvd gutter,
I spy my Leo horoscope
between the inky thighs
of the *L.A. Express*
adorned by a tangle
of bushy words.

The incidental oracle
tells me to *speak out against*
those who oppress you,
but don't forget to employ
a touch of expressive diplomacy,
and just as I finish
scrying the last line,
a behemoth #733
comes roaring to a stop
and my slutty seeress
gets caught up
in the undercarriage.

As the bus pulls away,
her papery arm
waves a pathetic farewell,
and I'm now left
to choose the better
of two phrases,
"sincere kara
i ne donas damninda,"
or *"kisi mian pugon."*

Little Bombadiers

The early risers
who sip coffee,
fold towels,
and hang up
button-down collared shirts
on plastic hangers
don't notice
the row of pigeons
strung on an electrical wire
above the laundromat,
the fully-stocked
soap dispensers,
or change machines
ready to accept
their hard-earned cash,
until they arrive home
to find a Kandinsky
or Rorschach masterpiece
on their clean clothes.
And so, they make their way
back to the laundromat,
now crowded
with working mothers
and truckloads of wash,
pause beneath
phone wire
now empty
of little bombardiers
and wonder...
and *wonder...*

HELEN LOSSE

Today a message comes (to us)

all the way from Heaven—
wearing the mouth of Maya Angelou,
her bright lipstick
smiling through her white flash of teeth—

to remind us how phenomenal it will be
when we all are able to tell each other:
It is always best when we sing together
and with the angels.

BRUCE McCANDLESS

As I Watch You Get Dressed

They'll pay for this. The old
and all the old at heart, bookkeepers of their own disappointment,
draining their accounts as fast as they can.
Now—today—with the scent of your hair on my belly,
the licorice taste of your tongue on my lips,
I want to pull the floor up over our heads.
I want this afternoon to loop itself around a sturdy year
and hang there, like wisteria, but it can't.
People at bus stops are checking their phones.
They're taking small notes. They're shoving our hours down stairs,
herding the minutes like guards in a gulag and
soon, if we're not careful, soon
our thumbs will start to shrivel.
Plants will die. My shoes will crack. So I
intend to hide inside us. Burn all bridges. Eat the key.
Our studies require further study.
We are formulating certain theorems essential to
the soft geometry of repetitive coupling.
We are making mythologies of muscle and sweat.
I therefore intend to utter no sound but the sound of your name and
hope tomorrow misplaces our home address.
Maybe next week will miss its connecting flight.
Maybe the future will get lost like an old man in the frozen foods as
we feed each other naked oranges, and let
the sweet juice trickle—slowly; slowly—
down our chins.

BRUCE McCANDLESS

To a Friend of Average or Possibly Slightly Elevated Testosterone Levels, On His Wedding Day

You beam at her as she walks down the aisle and
swear to God you'll never go.
As if your words could make it so. Truth is,
all men hunger all the time for comely interns; accolades;
for flying lessons and foreign cars.
Every average morning's another arrow—one more proof
you'll leave no legend. You pluck it out.
By the time you hit the Kirkwood Exit you've
outwitted Osama, captured a number of Somali pirates,
stopped somewhere west of Laramie
the senseless bullying of ministers and aging dogs.
At work you storm whole ranks of mortgage banks,
fight for provinces of ergonomic chairs.
Achievement almost ends it. But does not.
Consider Alexander weeping on the plains of Punjab,
his spearmen muttering and sore,
all the east unveiled and no more worlds to win.
How long could coves hold gray Odysseus
before he fell through doors again,
found himself full-scream again, chasing doubts across the sea?
Achievement almost ends it. But does not.
The fighting outlasts what is fought.
And you, wind chaser, king of cold calls,
I'm tossing you this wreath of words
to wish you blessings that you don't deserve:
that she'll consent to rule your restless heart
and wait for you where autumn starts;
then take your heavy year-scarred hands
and lead you home to quiet lands.

JENNIFER A. McGOWAN

Callisto

The hazy memory of heat.
The shimmer of first frost.
October.
Two duvets and hot chocolate.
In the north, the Great Bear
circles her son, the way
my thoughts return to you.
Clear and crystallized.

Dead leaves rustle and wilt.
A last dead petal of rosa rugosa,
blown against the window,
slides in a damp streak
and tears.
Flowers left too long
in a vase, water cloying and fetid—
an inner echo.

I am old
and full of sleep, but I long
for the sight of you, bright shock
of gray in your hair making
you look like a history don
erring on the side of tweed
and jeans, just to be safe.

My eyes are empty. My arms.
Outside the wind keens and kills.
Walpurgisnacht. The dead dance.
I set lanterns for you, knowing
you will never descend.
In your shadow I shiver. Night thickens.
Ghosts sing through my mind,

yours foremost. A litany of loss.
A lesson in survival.
The hazy memory of heat;
the shimmer of frost.
The Great Bear circles.
My thoughts return to you.
Intact. Incandescent. Unholy.

Child's Play

We grew up hard.
We acted like children.
After school
we played school.
I carved my name
on the desk of my flesh.
I wrote mash notes
to Mary Jo Talarico's
cotton panties.
Miss Duke
had a solid set of gams,
shapely calves
in silky hose.
I wanted to touch her.
I wanted to reach out
and run one finger
into Neverland.
Love was getting the strap
for talking back.
Love was detention,
our not-so-secret rendezvous.
I wanted to make babies,
little baby babies,
however that happened.
Like homework.

Old Family Recipe

It all goes into the cauldron.
A three-headed dog-hair.
Splinters from the true cross.
The world's fastest turnip.
Uncle Remus's gall bladder.

Stir with a few well-chosen words.
Season with sorrow.
Add a pinch of angel's buttocks.
A tablespoon of teaspoons.
Some salt of the earth.

Simmer, like a bad temper.
Stew over the past awhile.
And lastly, the secret ingredient,
a dash of midnight.
Served cold and without question.

JACQUELINE MARKOWSKI

She Would Not Even Discuss Hospice

when they offered her weeks
to live and said she was too sick
to get well. She was sick enough
for constant euphoria, delivered
by transdermal patches. Soon they
covered her torso
like an airmail package, enough
postage to carry her home again.

The nurses were patient. They knew
I was moving in before I did, that I had
given up on sleep, would forgo
the comfort of coffee and fresh air
without urging. They knew I carried
the weight of it, that I was dying,
too. I floated down their hallways,
broaching non sequiturs, hugging
anyone who didn't run, begging
for tales of other tragedies to escape
our present.

The case managers took me seriously
when I said there was nowhere else
to go. Those pant-suited, short-haired
menopausal angels looked
through their thick glasses, saw need
in my eyes, or in the lids of my mother's.
They were like nuns, kind, lonely smiles,
always hushed, hands cold from constant
washing. They lived on the sidelines of stories
like ours for decades. In the evenings
they pulled away, leaving the hospital,
going home to the absence
of beeping monitors,

negative space of grown children,
refrigerators feathered by the art of long
distance grandchildren, mantles crowded
with yellowed thank you cards from mourning
daughters just like me.

TODD MERCER

Blanche DuBois's Kind Strangers

Hindsight sifts the conscientious
from the grifters she stumbled around with
as the family farm declined, the legacy
slipped into disrepair. A few
exceptional friends and beaus
kept her confidences, though they
had to leave her in their order,
none could persevere. A handful
over leaner years saw her cover herself
with naiveté, the defense against a century
so fast, perplexing. A life mis-spent
and well-spent on searches
for the merciful.

The Dream Thief

where are the dream pageants of our grandmothers and grandfathers when
colorful as birds carefree as birds they ascended

— *Zbigniew Herbert, trans. Alissa Valles*

Insidious noticed the days had gotten shorter,
dark as his bedroom with the lights
out—the clock off, candle
wick dry, stiff as a dead anemone.
Someone came in and stole his happiness.
His thoughts were wild
horses spooked by the field's hooked
padding, clouded-moon grass.
Cold out there and honestly,
he mused, my thoughts are out of control.
They are circus bears and lions, my head
in their mouths. How could he
have known adulthood brought such
misery, that one's own mind
could betray everything, ruin the country
of his very life, his sleep.

There is a faery who steals dreams,
makes a changeling of locomotive horns,
crimps them in a box and
plants it in the brain. After all,

after all this...the Bodhisattva wrestles himself—
because someone left a canoe in the river—
empty, crowded, moonlit.

Letter Written to His Brother Theo from Vincent Van Gogh

Imagine me
    in my studio
        next to the open window
my easel propped up
    in the corner a shaft of light
highlighting the canvas.

I'm painting the blues of the sky,
       the blues of the world
outside my window
    the world inside my soul,
swirling the blues to reflect
the music inside me.
       Music everywhere.
    I see paintings
in poorest cottages,
    dirtiest corners.

Paint splatters my clothing.
I could step inside my work,
    walk
the verdant greens
    of the field.

ANDERSON O'BRIEN

To Frida Kahlo on Reading Her Diary

Frida, amiga, I want to leap
into the pages of your journal

        my body burning

like yours:
      strings of random
           words
      dark, mismatched
           pearls.

You were shattered,
      your spine jagged,
pain beyond all bearing,
           stains splattering your pictures,
setting forth yellow as the color
      of madness,

telling of your love for Diego,
      the kind of love you bite into
           like an apple, bruises and all.

But I see you, Frida,
not a broken-
           winged sparrow,
but a quetzal, resplendent
      in throaty greens and reds.

ANNE BRITTING OLESON

The Music of the Spheres

Fractured sound waves gather themselves
at the tip of the car antenna
somewhere along route 7 after nightfall.

I pass through the smallest of towns,
shut down at nine o'clock,
thinking of the music that forms
of waves or particles

and which I can only imagine must exist
in the head of the teenaged boy,
backlit in the silent storefront,
dancing with a mop
as I drive by, more alone, even, than he.

SHAWNTE ORION

When Asked What Kind of Cult I Grew Up In

It was the kind of cult secluded in the woods.
Isolated from neighbors and sin.

The kind of cult that believes Saturday
is the new Sunday and it should start
on Friday night.

The kind of cult that believes death is a sleep
where you dream of nothing
while the wicked get a snooze button
for an extra millennium.

The kind of cult that believes Jesus
will return on October 22nd 1844.
The kind of cult that could be wrong.

The kind of cult that spawned
extremist offshoot cults of vegetarians,
Branch Davidians and breakfast cereals.

The kind of cult that needed my mother
to sew handmade extensions
onto the bottoms of felt dresses
worn by little felt women
on the felt pages of my activity book
so I wouldn't be seduced
by impure desires.

But I had already found salvation
in the flesh of real ankles
attached to the legs of real women.
Legs that could be felt
all the way up to heaven.

SHAWNTE ORION

Good Housekeeping Seal of Approval

The view of clouds through her window
holds the wall in place

as a flurry of kisses settles in the frigid
snowglobe of her mother's marriage

while all of the dead
skin cells & hair fragments,

mites feeding on micro fibers
of food & the dander of other mites,

translated as dust along the floorboards
will soon exist in a vacuum.

JAMES OWENS

Poem on His Birthday

At midnight wind scoured the sky,
chasing fine dust and the stiff leaves

of a dry November, the year's corner
where air caught and was torn.

All night he wanted to think about wind,
not the unexpected life that had taken him

as if lurking in a blind sector of sky,
driving the past into its wake,

demanding the assumption of gray evenings,
when, even with the warm lover beside him,

he would rise and step through heavy rooms.

He desired wind itself above the house,
not wind as metaphor, as if a river

of days slid across the empty sky.
Perhaps there would be a storm.

When the clock twitched and clicked,
he augured rain lavish on the roof

and stripped branches lashed and wild
for miles all through the dark country.

That's not all—he wanted morning, wet and shining,
twigs from the ruined choirs,

little particulars, that kind of paradise.

SCOTT OWENS

Rapture

As soon as Sara saw the room she knew
she had to do it here, buck-naked
writhing on polished hardwood, surrounded
by the sounds and sights of mortal sin
in reds and yellows, snakes and hearts,
tears and flame, all the signs
of man's perdition, and the bright white
hope of something worth rising for.

She touched herself every time
she went inside, lingered a little
longer, waiting, growing eager,
knowing it was just a matter of time
before the right man would come along,
and she knew it was him right away,
blue suit and black book,
cane handle gripped in one hand.

She guided him in and down almost
in one motion, and when he did
taste and see he feared nothing,
he loved life, he exalted, he was delivered.
And keeping him always on her lips
she pulled from him praise and rejoicing,
and glorifying again and again until
all that was left was alleluia.

Forbearance

His father leaving before he was born wasn't enough.
Hand-me-down clothes, shoes with the toes cut out,
The lack of a third, sometimes a second meal couldn't do it.
Belt buckles, stove tops, locked closets, hands
On faces were only temporary reasons for doubt.
The uncle bleeding out from his left ear
On the living room floor, the grandfather's body
Consuming itself, the familiarity of hatred,
Of use and abuse, judgment, disapproval,
Condemnation, not even the pressures of sin
and all their wages combined could keep him from believing.
More weight, he said, shaking a fist at God.

Stains

I had not visited this farm for years as I walked
along logging roads where I had watched trucks
loaded with great oak and pine climb
and descend the hills. I could see clear
as opening morning the myopic buzzards
wheeling above me, and coming towards me
billowing brown leaves that blew across
the twisting road. Fescue waved where Charolais
and Jersey grazed under the shade of a walnut tree.
On the ground, abandoned by white-faced squirrels
declining to defile margins of their furred mouths,
black hulls of walnuts lay. I was the boy
who tore open their dark pulp and between
two stones cracked the ebony ridged shells,
picking down to the heart of reticulated meat.
As I walked this path, edged by chickweed
and blackberry brambles, the sun suddenly
burst upon me between the branches
of the walnut trees, my blemished hands
holding an indelible sweetness of stains.

Miners

I looked up Coal Town,
Pennsylvania, and found
the town was gone,
though green hills stayed.
Where anthracite
was picked and shoveled,
elevators had lowered
men wearing lanterns
and holding caged birds.
Coal smudged faces
would rise up from pits
only to descend
into blacker chambers,
trees of their lungs
dark as the black
filling up graves.
Though I don't crawl
through tunnels of earth
digging diamonds or coal,
and may walk across fields
of wild strawberries and buttercups
shining in sunlight beside lakes
where white ducks and swans float,
not thinking of coal dust
or lost towns where children
once wove chains of clover,
all this will be gone, and after I
have ceased speaking will anyone
search for my words as I
have sought this abandoned mine?

Two Brown Knots

A slight knock. Is it the door? I open it. No one is there.
On the boards of the porch two round knots like the eyes
in a Japanese cartoon. We are hardwired to recognize faces.
I see a face. If I stare at it, will it begin to move? I have

heard it said that if you look at a painting long enough,
it will start moving. Ships will sail. Flowers will waver
in a slight breeze. The nude will descend the staircase.
I hope the face will speak to me, bring me a message

from another dimension. It is no burning bush, but it
will suffice. She asks me, *What are you looking at?*
I point to the two brown knots. *Maybe it's him.* She
is wiser than I am, *It can't be him,* but she stares along

with me. A feather from the mourning dove killed by
a red-tailed hawk yesterday floats across the porch.
Who can distinguish between a sign and a random act?
Is it the knots or the feather I should listen to?

LEE PASSARELLA

A Tree Lovely as a Poem

You see the signs, these late-October mornings,
where the oak has wrestled beauty from the cold.
Some angel's bestowed blessings made of gold
(while TV, empty-handed, blares freeze warnings).

Its leaves read like the map of an invasion.
Or no—a tomographic image of the brain:
here lie the verdant valley and cool plain
where gray cells take their ease, in hibernation,

and there, in lava flows, you see it waking—
a Kilauea spreading to the coast—
thoughts welling up, the mind about to roast
in red-hot symbols of its fabricating.

LEE PASSARELLA

In a Rothko Landscape

Late October, Donegal Springs, Pennsylvania

Cows low, invisible in a fog as thick
as soup base: milk and water. Their voices
are immediate, cupped in the dense-wet

air, offered as a fact you can't avoid,
their smell ripe as an ancient barnyard
in this airless bell of vapor. Even the leaves

are milked of their savor, fall as sound only,
amplified. Near the eponymous springs,
a dump of broken mailboxes, packing cases,

the dark bones of departed farm tools.
And in the angle of the fence, a yellow
chaise, almost new—a front-row seat

to nothing. It is a canvas of white and
black, with one screaming-yellow smudge,
lacking the complacency of any sorrow.

Untitled (1)

from Old Man Poems

The best sermon I ever preached
Was the very first one.
I can remember the musty smell
Of the carpet, the murphy oil
On the oldoak altar,
The fragrant pine casket,
The sickening spray of flowers,
And I remember how the pastor
I assisted, about to begin his message,
Buckled over with grief,
And everyone's eyes lifted
Toward me, to see what words
I had for a manI had not known.
I could barely feel my feet
In the pulpit and the words
Rolled right out of my mouth
Like a player piano scrolling.
I spoke about love and honor,
Faith and humility. I referenced
A miracle and a parable
And I felt the light from a
Stained glass window
Bathing my face in purple,
And I knew at twenty-two
This was what I was born to do.

Untitled (2)

from *Old Man Poems*

I wrote this poem
with my piss in the woods
in the dry leaves beneath
the red maple canopy
where god can't see
and the snakes don't care
and i'm thinkin about the people
thinkin about the people
never gonna make it
never gonna be more
though they get up every morning
every cold foggy morning
and they do what they're told
and they hold their backs straight
but they're never gonna make it
never gonna make it
though they carry our trash
and they clean our forks
and they watch our kids
and they cook our steaks
they are never gonna make it
never gonna make it
so I wrote this pome
across a page in the woods
for their doomed dull eyes
and their broken down feet
and their tired aching backs
because god can't see
and the snakes don't care.

FREDERICK POLLACK

Nice

Inspired by a somewhat sentimental
but well-made film, he decides
to forgive wrongs and wrongdoers
from his early life. (He wonders in what way
he is forgiving people, not just
images; but the question is disturbing and
unanswerable.) He experiences,
as moralists predict, disorientation:
children he had seen
as huge malignant forms are reduced
to children, grownups to confused and frightened
kids. There is a sense of greater range.

But where can he go in it? He's old,
now. He might show with less effort
an interest in uninteresting
people he meets, if he meets anyone.
Be known for equanimity, humility,
which actually are required of the old
if they get out at all. (Thus he imagines
his scrap of future.) He will make
unsought and unperceived amends.
An eggshell light bathes
the contents of his mind, which feel
as trivial as the external world.

Emergency Room Visit in Early Summer

I'm ten minutes in to an asthma treatment
a couple is assigned to the curtain next to me

I listen to a woman in her early thirties
her broken language
moaning
keening
frantically pointing to her stomach
"water, too much water"

the nurse asks for a Chinese translator over the intercom
the woman still moaning
"eight pounds, eight pounds"

finally her husband
smoothes out the words she cannot say
"she hasn't peed in three days"
"she is retaining eight pounds of water"

when the doctor finally arrives
the husband explains...
"she was diagnosed with stomach cancer Monday
they're starting chemo on Friday"

fifteen minutes later,
the woman is quiet
and serum is delivered in silent millimeters

his hands pull back her damp hair
and I wonder how a dialect
can spread across a room so fast

at midnight I am told I can leave,
the air outside has cooled
—finally enters my lungs without regret

I pause before I get into the car
and think about how from this moment
he will dream of her
before there was water

The Night Before Surgery

Take the dog
on a long walk

the one where you pass
the old metal bridge
beyond the area
marked with "mud slide" signs

watch his footsteps carefully
and he will help you
find the places
to hide
when you
enter that long
languid
journey of anesthesia

watch the way
his fur mingles
with the slight breeze
how he follows the faint edges
of a gravel path

feel the cadence
the rise and fall of his lungs
and tell him
you will see him there
on the ledge of solitude
and remember
he will teach you
everything about the anaphora
that stays in the body
that stays beneath your skin
only as apparent
as faded scar tissue
or mercy

A Conversation on the Balcony in Panama City Beach about Crow-fly Distance

It wasn't the car that moved us.
A change of mindset
proves it's the wheels that turned
the planet and pulled the white
sand of the Emerald
Coast to our toes,
the miles bunched up behind us
like ribbon on the floor
after opening presents.

Imagine a flight from east coast to west
as a dotted line from one end of the moon
to another, an X in the middle for a plane.

Who ever considers the center of the moon
is a thousand miles closer to us than the edges?

This means we are far
too trusting: that wine
doesn't come from pressed butterfly
wings, that timeshares won't collapse
in the Gulf once we're asleep,
that the Earth won't pull
itself apart scratching the itch
of all the cars spinning it.

STEPHEN ROGER POWERS

Limeade for Echo & the Bunnymen

Yesterday I juiced eight
limes, boiled most of the sugar
left, ran the faucet for six and a half
cups of water, and added a teaspoon
of salt the way the Thai
cookbook told me.

The salt made the first sip
quite a pucker, so I poured
a bottle of Bud Lite Lime in the pitcher
to Americanize it to something more
like a margarita.

With her vodka-frosted head
on my chest, my girlfriend listened to me
drink it. She said it sounded like
Gullfoss Waterfall in Iceland thawing
and trickling to a splash down
at the end of a dark cave. Listen:

when unpaid gas bills freeze
the living room, album covers
are the best travel brochures.

Neighbors

There is a man made of papier-mâché.
I do not mean a piece of art.
I do not mean a representation.
The man is made of papier-mâché
And he lives.
He sits on the edge of his crumpled bed
And ponders his papier-mâché toes.
He adjusts his unpaginated pajama top
Over his stubble-covered papier-mâché chest.
He contemplates getting dressed.
The day stretches out before him,
A black and white montage
Of ordinary deeds, a succession of tasks
That lead him, by the functioning
Of his papier-mâché heart and
Papier-mâché lungs and papier-mâché
Liver, from one station to the next,
Each existential encounter an opportunity
To leave, as well as take, residue: ending
Eventually back at a comfortable home. He thinks:
If only it were raining today.
I catch him peering around his curtain,
The clear day's reflections interleaved
With his face and inarticulate papier-mâché
Hand and I am sorry for him.
This morning I think we will speak.
This morning I think, with smooth to rough,
We will awkwardly shake hands,
My dry skin alleging the first abrasion of his friendship.

Quality of Birth

It is time
For the woman's child.
She is taken to a cabin
At the rough edge of the village:
One where the roof rises
Not as high as all the others
And the fence outside
Is in need of consensual repair.
Normally, villagers complete their time
In the dark concern of their own
Mumbling homes, with a mid-wife,
And the presumed father fiercely restricted
To another, less important room.
This woman
Has no such attendants:
The father is unknown.
One wanting night three men
From the village next
Caught this woman alone doing
Her family's spent laundry,
A means to an end littering the riverside,
And made of her, in her own suspicious telling,
Unwilling breeding stock. This
To her is no welcomed child. To the house
At the border of civilization
She goes to be delivered. Her hands
Devour each other, and her smell is
Of deceit and devaluation. Not even
This child should be raised
By a mother so easily shamed.
Our village takes note not
Because there is joy or welcoming,
But because the process is noisy.

So when you stand
Do not knock out your hips
Like an opening gate; keep
Your clarion hair under dull cloth;
Pull down the traitorous ends of your shirt.
None of us want to end up
With her: wrong time,
Right remedy.

KEN POYNER

One Mermaid, After the Tsunami

I came home
To splinters and fresh sand;
To door frames on their sides;
To kitchen chairs in tree limbs;
To a woman's nightgown,
Dry now,
Spread like a rumor of swimming
Across the broken finality
Of the salt-poisoned bushes.
The water has made away,
Taking less property than taking
The organization of property,
Washing randomness into the landscape
Of ordinary patterns.
A window frame reclined
In a sideways easy chair;
Ruined bread in a teddy bear's lap.

I see you half way
Through the survey of my foundering damage.
My pool, holding in its mouth
All the rogue ocean water it could swallow:
And you: you, and families of stray
Community lawn furniture;
My pool, gap toothed and agape, once
Chlorinated, once smiling with fresh water,
Now holding the gift of aftermath.
So, the ocean tossed you out.
Don't think of suffering sympathy from me.
Just wait until I get down
To my bathing trunks.

DAVID RADAVICH

At a Scenic Park

Men drive up
at high speeds
with nowhere to go,

their pick-ups
washed,
fully loaded.

No war,
no damsel
in distress.

The lake
ripples
gently.

Big tires,
tow-holds
mean readiness.

Off they go
having done
enough
for one day.

DAVID RADAVICH

Memories Are Smart

They run home
like children on the street.

They know how
to escape from danger

and hide
deep in the bush.

That town I lived in
with its hills and highrises

still has creeks
I visit and recognize.

That face
is still young

that I coveted.

Everything knows
when to stay in its place.

Even the dog barks
next door

as if the mailman
could deliver

that long-
missing check.

Beatitude

Purple drifts of myrtle blooms
plucked off by the squall
edge the muddy street as Lulah walks
the last few steps from Highland
to the trolley stop—

not one of their better visits,
with Vi so eked of spirit
she seemed translucent
as powdered milk and water
when Lulah gets proportions wrong.

Tales of new kittens could not rouse her,
nor a pocketful of rhymes
nor buttercups bundled
with juniper sprigs and fairywand,
to tide her through the next moon.
The kingdom of heaven
may be Vi's one day, but no time soon—

Crackling on its wire,
the trolley stops before her and she boards.
As the driver rings the bell,
a rush of blossoms startles from the trees.

Contraband

The White Army had rummaged
through her cache again,
discovered Lulah's hankie
full of althaea and agrimony,
pine needles and plantain leaf,
sacrificed the lot to compost.

To cloak anything well in such a cell,
too small even for a proper chest—
even for sunlight, most days—
required more cunning
than she laid claim to,
and those women could out-sly
a skulk of foxes.

Vidalia half-smiled; the plantain leaf
was Lulah's little joke,
its power to thwart marauding hands
more superstition than truth.
But the others she'd have found use for,
to counterjinx the mutterings
of the frost-lipped nurses, stiff as meringues

in their uniforms, or to attract
the benevolent spirits
that surely, even here, in this sad refuge
on a hill, could ease the thoughts
of wayward reason, and scour hearts
like hers, petrified to stone,
till they gleamed.

Killing Time

I watch the traffic
reduced from four lanes to two.
The far lanes are scraped and rough
lined with orange cones
splattered with tar.

A work crew in hard hats
and fluorescent yellow vests
sweat in the heat , repaving the road,
driving pint-sized bulldozers and rollers,
shoveling, raking, sweeping,
waving cars through red lights
where the cross streets are blocked.

Two guys wait for the tattoo parlor to open.
John's Kitchen is busy with breakfast.
It's the only place I know that serves brains
and chitlins in this neighborhood.

A girl primps in the pawn shop window.
My coffee gets cold too fast but that's okay.
It's hot as hell and I'm waiting to meet
somebody down the block.

I sold my trumpet there.
The pawn shop guy with the gun on his hip
actually gave me what I paid for it
because I asked way too much.
I put gas in my car.

Now I'm looking to sell something else
but not my guitar
and never my dignity.

JONATHAN K. RICE

Pennies in a Urinal

I stood at a urinal
in the men's room

at my favorite café.

Unzipped myself
when I noticed

three pennies in the drain.

I hesitated but had to go.
Thought maybe someone made a wish

but with no fountain
or wishing well nearby

he chose the urinal instead.

Maybe he made three wishes
or a political statement.

I live in the South

so pissing on Lincoln
would make sense.

I wanted to remove them
but I couldn't bring myself to reach in.

I flushed the blue water and piss.
The green tinted liquid

swirled down the drain.
The pennies remained.

I left them where I found them
Lincoln firm and resolute.

P. R. RICE

Wellingtons

The August dawn brings
Showers scattered in some

Morphine haze. Puddles, now
Breeding on the split-vein

Streets, mark the passing time,
Are disrupted by a girl

Stomping on their watch top
Faces in her pink

Marshmallow Wellingtons.

P. R. RICE

Shadow

Sometimes your shadow
Enters the room, not

You but a rampant trace
Cutting through lamp

Shade measures on the
Still mostly bare

Walls. At that time
I'm glad I still sleep

With the phone by the
Bed because

I swear you'll call
Even though I don't

Have a land line
Anymore

MARY RICKETSON

Absent

Those old live oaks look like battered women now.
I remember them draped in fine Spanish moss,
branches hanging to the ground,
grand curtsy to all comers by.
Welcome home to Biloxi, one always said
in a long southern drawl,
Take off you shoes, feel the sand between your toes,
Watch the evening sun sink down into the Gulf.
Typically I obeyed without hesitance,
then sank my teeth into hush puppies,
steamed shrimp, and stuffed flounder.
Later I'd wile away the hours with Daddy,
he in one rocker and me in the other,
no particular things to say.

Everything changed when a great storm fisted up,
beat the living daylights
out of every tree along the coastal edge.
Naked and blown, branches broke to the stub.
Only raw strength and basic beauty remains,
in the absence of Spanish moss.

Today, after the funeral,
a few gulls whisper as the tide comes in.
A sad refrain overshadows my own grief.
My live oaks will survive.
In time their limbs will reach out
to hug me when I come back.
But the Spanish moss is absent
and Daddy's chair is empty.

Pruning Time

I've never done this before,
never cut out unneeded parts.
These thirty year blueberry plants,
nine feet high, are too tall
to pick without a ladder,
too dense and matted for sun
to reach every limb.

I have to do this, sacrifice the size
of these mother bushes,
improve the yield, make the harvest.
I have to discard part of the last many years.

Hand clippers, long handled loppers
and a good eye at my command,
I plunder through a maze of dormant limbs.
Prune no more than one third of each bush,
I repeat like a mantra,
the only thing I know for sure,
then circle each one four times,
looking for what I have missed.

Often surprised or confused,
something comes clear.
I've always done this,
cut out parts of life
that no longer function.

KATHERINE RIEGEL

What Is Tender Must Hide

By the Gulf I watched the shallow waves
bring them up on the sand—
a hundred coquina shells like marbles,
blue, yellow, orange, pink,
purple memory of pain,
green of lost
joy. I walked the threshold,
my feet cold in winter water.
The shells were a mosaic
people would pay to see
after thousands of years. And then—
I had not known they were alive
inside—they dug themselves
down into the sand.

Criminals

I'm not sure you understand.
When a kingfisher dies, I fall
into dark water, my feathered heart
dwindling down to ash; and part of me
wants to burn down
the human world until every
last one of us is dead
so the animals
can be safe at last.
Who am I
to rage so, when I am
also the hunter
carrying, somewhere
in his body,
a furred thing, cowering?
Oh, my fellow criminals,
let it be the end
of this play. Let's take off our human suits
and scamper off on our paws
before the songless morning comes.

The Hitchhiker

sits in my car.
He has the beauty
of fear;
we both wonder
if we will kill
each other,
deaths like editing,
the lonely sharp
realization
that we may never make
the fence
so far in the distance,
the car overturning
like God on fire
and us thrown
into the stupidity
of man's need
for burning
desperately
away from any sense
of boredom
or peace.

The Rings

You sell yours
before either of us can pack
and leave.

I keep mine, wear it
for months after the house
is sold,
keep it in a soft
blue
pouch,
waiting for the day I need
cash
more than I need
to keep
my promise.

SUSAN ROOKE

Fifteen Years Ago

She called again to tell me
World War III had broken out;
the end was near. Somewhere
havoc had a nation by the throat—
this time bombs, or gas, or town squares
slippery with blood. Every night
the news wheezed sulfur from the TV set

into her lightless, grimy rooms.
She misconstrued it, the way she'd started
misconstruing her house keys and her car.
What set her off that night
I don't remember, but I still recall
the grim "I-told-you-so" on her end
of the phone, the smugness too,

because she did grasp that being right
about anything at all was important
now that her discernment was swamped
and lying at the bottom of a deep, cold sea.
So I listened, feeling queasy, knowing
she was right about the end,
however much she misconstrued.

SUSAN ROOKE

Witching for Water

When he called the water came running,
up from the dust, the stones, each time
he resorted to the magic in his hands, in the fork
cut from a young green tree. After willow,

fruit trees were the best, he said, needing so much
water that they knew where to find it, as if a red X
marked the spot there on the ground. But if
a fruit tree wasn't handy, he used whatever was,

something young and flimsy, slender-limbed.
Drowning in sand the land could be, mesquite
hissing its dry gossip on the hot wind, but he saw it
differently, saw pastures knee-deep in water,

drinking in a sweet flood. I remember his face
thoughtful, looking into the mind of water, feeling
in his bones where it plunged and frothed in the blind
channels beneath our feet. He'd unfold his penknife

from its ivory case, cut a slim fork from a sapling,
flex it in his calloused palms. He'd take his grip,
underhand, then pace to the slow rhythm
of a young tree's heart. And when he found water,

as he always did, he'd pass the fork to me, just
seven years old, but old enough to feel the pulse
beating in the wood, to draw water like
the moon does, calling with my hands the tides.

The Blind

When the Nile rose to fifty-seven feet
and all of Egypt festered under water,

Pheros, son of Sesostris, came to power.
During his reign he won no wars.

A simple act of arrogance brought him fame:
he hurled his spear at the river,

insensed that it would flood. And on the spot
he was struck blind. Ten years he lived that way,

but in the eleventh he met an oracle
who told him if he washed his eyes with urine

from a Buto City woman who'd never
slept with any man except her husband,

his vision would return. He tried his only wife,
and when that failed he had to try

all the Buto wives. Imagine those women
sitting patiently, cup in hand,

each planning out her future, the wife of Pheros
gathering the cups, dipping a swab in each,

then dobbing it into his blinking eyes.
Imagine too the stench of different urines

streaming through his beard, his growing fear
the oracle had lied. And when the last one's urine

washed away his blindness, he declared
he'd marry her, invited all the rest

inside the palace walls, had them bound
and set ablaze. How could the oracle

let this happen? Didn't he see the flames
lapping bodies, wrapping each one gently,

lifting their ashes to the gods, were the lovers
he'd divined? And what about this wife,

his new one, how could she face the others?
Happy, yes, but would she see the difference

once the shimmering Nile receded.

JUDITH SKILLMAN

This Sadness Is No One's

It belongs to the white chicken,
and the child-woman
whose mother had fetal alcohol syndrome,
to the gray hulk of sky.

It is neither yours nor mine,
nor the woman who works
in the bakery or the post office
or the jewelry store.

This sadness lingers in a tone
of wood, in trains bulleting
from west to east.
It is vacancy enlarged with winter.

What you hold
isn't warm or alive. It doesn't cluck,
pick grubs from mud,
or strut around the yard

as if to impress.
This is the solitary watch.
Take the gun, the magnet,
the trick of hands without cards.

Ah Vallejo,

After you left Peru forever,
you made of guano Trilce,
that stands on the border
of every season.

The brick of time
sits between us.
I hold these pages
with the pure love
of a Hippodamia.

Drunken centaurs
come to abduct me,
they break me in two
in two as if I were
a simple straw.

Here on the island
of October, I mimic you
by copying your sadness.

Vallejo your materials remain
exiled as in a gallery
or a prison, those you
painted with terracotta
in the fine oils
of your Thursday.

ERIC STEINEGER

Reading Carl Sandburg, Drinking Newcastle

9:53 p.m.

I wonder Carl, if you ever came across a Newcastle.
Probably not, it didn't become available until 1928
and that was in England when it swept the awards.
But I'm sure you drank beer on occasion and laughed
like the dynamiter in one of your poems. You couldn't
have loved Chicago without enjoying an occasional beer.
Surely there was a table that got roughed up by
a good natured fist. Those shoulders.

If you were here, sitting across from me in this studio,
dressed in a plain grey jacket and folkloric tie, I would
tell you I see in you what you saw: the buffalo that are gone
and saw their end coming in that "great pageant of dusk."
Their "great heads," like your own end coming but who cares
when you have a wife named Paula with "only her drinking,
her night-grey eyes?"

12:47 a.m.

How long must we sit like this, Carl? There's a reason
I conjured you, though I'm curious *"Why North Carolina?"*
the only words you've blinked in the last hour in your
prairie posture, other than *"There's so many windows..."*
I know that you know I'm from North Carolina and you
lived in the town of Flat Rock, which is not far from
my alma mater in the mountains.... Can I offer you

a Newcastle? I'm not going to inquire your personal life
because apparently a nod is enough. But since you're here,
tremulous as a nail but friendly, tell me about the night
you wrote "Sunset from an Omaha Hotel Window."
When the last of the Midwestern sun faded behind
a few meager structures on the flat, flat land did you
just sit there—in the sill—in the darkness? Waiting
for sounds to come about?

TIM SUERMONDT

By the City

for Rachel

The sun shines like a blister
On the knee of a long ago childhood.

Pelicans and cranes fly over the harbor—
Adults on the pier toss hard-crusted breadcrumbs skyward.

A day so beautiful it's sad.
A day so sad it's beautiful.

What do we know of anything? Though we try.

The final loveliness of the night—
I see you coming.

down south

you don't slip into the south,
no—you tumble in head
first, catch your ankle
against gnarled roots,
crash through brambles
so sharp they rip through you,
land in creek water
cold enough to shiver
your bones clean in two.
quivering there in
shameless nakedness,
you wonder why
humanity stayed here
with the maggots, boars,
moss the color of a drowned
girl's hair. you wonder
why they ever claimed this
wild, sticky land for their own—
and then the song
reaches your ears,
low and sweet like hummingbirds.
you gather yourself and follow,
not knowing once you start
heading south, there's nowhere else
worth going but down.

ALICE TEETER

Old Oak Tree

The men have come to cut our odd oak tree.
They smoke beside their truck and eye the tree;
it leans too far, two forks, then canopy

with leaves, dense green, that blot the sky from sight.
The men blow smoke, the air is warm, they sight
the drops of branch or trunk, they scan the height

and walk this way. Their hands make counting signs,
their thumbs and fingers tap up dollar signs,
to climb our tree and take it down—two tines,

those round, huge trunks, are filled with wet, live wood.
They ask do we want them to haul the wood
or should they just pile it right where it stood?

This is our summer home, they live year round
and heat their homes with trees both bought and found.

The Pinched Pot

You stole a penny nail
from the hardware store
a bin full of them
sat out front

silver dazzling
sun glinting
gleaming

your hand flashed
over the wooden board
you pocketed it
deep in your dungarees
no one saw

the nail was sharp on the hand
and you worried the tip
with your thumb

you went to look
at the kittens and puppies
in their metal cages
at the back

you waited
your mother shopped

you carried the nail for years
always meant to pay
or return

the store has closed
the building is gone
you leave it on the ground
in the empty lot
the only shiny thing around

ALARIE TENNILLE

Layoff

It feels like divorce.
While you popped open
anniversary champagne,
your spouse changed
the locks, siphoned off
the accounts, left you
for a younger model.

You've slipped off the axle
of expectation, skidded
into an alternate universe,
wrecked in a pileup that took
out half your friends.

You wake from that familiar
dream of going to work naked
to find yourself stripped
of skin and ego. What to do?

You imitate your smile, pump
up your résumé, and tell the mirror
it's only a job.

ADEN THOMAS

My Grandmother's Hair

During the day she laced it into layers
of delicate lightnings and monochromes
(it took several hours, some would later say),
and tucked it from the world with bobby pins.

It slept above the white sheets of her neck,
feral, nocturnal, and a silver gray. It waited.
Not even the prairie wind could stir
from slumber its kinetic tendrils there.

On weekend nights when she would let it free,
it tumbled down to her toes in silver waves,
waves away from a decade on the sands,
and drowned the time along her hardwood floors.

The years have gone. Her porcelain ring box sits
atop my daughter's silver dresser drawers.
The bobby pins are stored inside. If I lean close
I feel that ocean crashing into shores.

ALLISON THORPE

Summer Storm, 1958

The storm rose early
with crow black drama,
snatching leaves and limbs,
swirling and yanking and whipping—
a mad scientist in the yard—
plucking curbside garbage cans and
throwing them like a tantrumed child,
ripping into neighborhoods
like a dog into a fresh-dug bone,
a delinquent student tearing up
a bad report card,
roaring and snarling
like a lion over bloodied meat.

Fearful and excited we watched
the spectacle from an upstairs window.

A sudden shudder killed the electricity,
mother rushing us to the basement,
lighting a thousand candles along the way,
prayers fierce under her breath.

Father came home early,
reporting the town in hiding.
He swung a lantern from a hand
roughened with roof work
and shadowed tobacco yellow.

When my sister started crying,
he sang *What a Friend We Have in Jesus*;
when she stopped sobbing,
he sang *Purple People Eater* and *Peggy Sue.*

We didn't often see him like this:
unmarred by drink and hate.
Deep in our stomachs it startled us
almost as much as the storm.

Mother gingerly opened the big freezer,
eyebrows a knitted question,
and brought out ice cream sandwiches.
We laughed as I stammered a ghost story
overheard at Corrine's slumber party.

Despite the rage and wrath of the day,
the destruction sent down to our world
by some furious sky warlord,
I filed those hours away in my thin album
of worthwhile family memories.

Years later, recalling that day was like
finding gold in the mashed potatoes,
a clean joke among dirty laundry,
a rainbow fanning the shuttered dark.

ALLISON THORPE

Reentering the World

for Al Stewart

Reentering the world
After winter's quarantine
Has loosed its clutch

Legs wobbled and puppy weak
I take to the wood trail
Feet fast recalling old steps

Sun's reach kind on my face
Wrens chippering news
From bush and fence

Trillium and bloodroot
Scattering the barren
Forest with their chant

Sky owning its color
Among the bleached
Fur face of clouds

Your ghost dashing
Tree to leafy tree
Like spring's autograph

JILL WHITE

The House Where I Learned to Breathe

The house where I learned to breathe is gone,
the family's archaeology
doomed beneath a screaming interstate.

The home on Rollins Avenue,
where *fresh* meant clean sheets off the line
and a smart-mouthed little girl;
where the rules of grown-ups reigned
but shifted and struck, random as lightning;
where corners and doors were constant
and I knew all the places it was safe to exhale.

The corner bungalow,
filled with all that hadn't happened yet,
prey to a pack of urban planners.

Like an arrow to the mark,
their new highway shot
straight through the little door
in the back of my closet
to the attic room
where, my sister told me,
God, and not the devil,
waited for me at night.

DANA WILDSMITH

Water

from "An Elemental Poem Cycle"

How They Travel Among Us

Fred's creek is a blue deepness
with silver streaks that dart and shift.
He stands sentinel in the rush of the culvert's suck,
plunging his kingly head under again and again,
his red tail a flag flapping in August swelter.
One morning, his mouth scoops a minnow.
He breaks rank, hopping to shore
to spit it at my feet.
Fred takes no prisoners.
When he dies,
he goes down hard,
a silken weight
slipping from my hands,
his creek a few breaths away.

Max begrudges the creek its right to hide his feet.
Dignity is all, and dignity abides on surfaces.
Creek water should be a cold drink,
nothing more than
a coolness to temper a dog meant to live in woods
more northern than ours.
But I am here in this hot country, so he agrees to be.
In trade for his dispensation of place,
however, I am to wait with patience
while he drinks. And drinks. And drinks.
I do.
Death comes to Max as a sneaky trick,
a fierce twisting of his belly's creeks and channels.
All along the hours of his last long night,
my hands skim his sleek black surfaces.

Lily watches from her brown chair
as Max goes under.

Later, we carry him to his deep bed by the creek.
I'm sorry, Max, I think. *I wish we could bury you higher.*
Lily turns away from my talking to dirt;
she jumps the creek's cooling October waters
and I jump after,
following her knotty rump
past the fern beds and up our oak hill
to where the deer wait.

DANA WILDSMITH

Fire

from "An Elemental Poem Cycle"

A car's tire whammed Lily's jaw
with one searing whack of realignment
that bumpered half her face
half an inch back.
Sleep always sets her to running again,
her front paws flopping against the recliner's tweed pavement,
gaining no distance from her history.
Look at me, Lily.
My hand slides under her jaw
to raise her head.
I didn't have you then.

My hand supporting Lily's head
is ancient with wrinkles
and has been since the night
I shook hands with fire
as it traveled up my nightgown
toward my face.
A fourteen-year-old wants no other destination
than the progress of her face
toward beauty,
so I gave my hands as fuel
to burn that fire out.

The heft of Lily's head
on my open palm
shifts from sleep
to trust.

Lily lolls her tongue sideways
to lick what's left of my little finger.

JOHN SIBLEY WILLIAMS

Parable

Half-way between window panes—
in the airless
self-contained universe
between outside
and in—
a spider explains life
in the long extinct language
of survival,
while a fly—entangled half-way
between firmament and glass—
struggles against understanding
that in digesting we become
the gods we seek
outside,

and as witness I
am still no closer to light
than a story
told in the unreflective space
between mirrors.

MARTIN WILLITTS, JR.

Letter to Caitlin, a Love Poem

Dylan Thomas met Caitlin Macnamara in 1936

1.

Do you remember the night we met
in the Wheatsheaf pub in London?
They say, when I laid my head on your lap I was drunk—
but I was really drunk with love.

You were a dancer who danced into my heart,
and there you shall dance forever.

No matter how many women they say
I would stray to like a lost dog,
I would return to you like an annual,
like a north star for a sailor,
like a lamp with blinding blue flame.

They say, I drunkenly proposed that night,
but I was staring into the swirl in your eyes.
I was swallowed into them, like a forthcoming,
like a sea swell in the orchestra of night,
and though I clung to the ropes of reality,
I let go into your face of pure light.

2.

Do you remember when we married in Penzance?
How we tore into each other like piñatas,
spilling our love on the counters, the bear rug,
the crystal chandelier casting diamond light in your hair?

We were stormy, drenching with star juice, moon halves,
almonds, and castaway fragments of belief.

And it was worth it, wasn't it, to burn like that?

3.

When I die, bury me in the churchyard in Laugharne.
Carry my casket like it was a bouquet of lilies.
Return my body to the earth where I shall kiss it.
Remember me when you look out at the sea.

MARTIN WILLITTS, JR.

Coda: Dylan Thomas and the Newspaper Article Found Inside His Wallet When He Died

When Dylan died,
he had one newspaper article about himself
folded in his wallet
like a black-lipped pearl oyster hides a black pearl.

It must have been special to him;
he carried it like a talisman
to every poetry reading, every hotel, every beach,
every corner meeting—
everywhere—his whole life.

It was a picture of him winning a footrace in school.
He would point at it and say,
Look, I was not always chubby.

But with Dylan, there were truths
and truths within truths
and he loved telling a great lie.

The truth is
it was a handicapped race.

No, he was not handicapped. It means something different.

He was expected to run a mile track
and he had a three-quarter head start.

All through his life he would find short cuts—
don't we all?

Here was Dylan proud of his one accomplishment
that had zilch to do with poetry:
it was about accomplishment.

MARTIN WILLITTS, JR.

Harmony on Fern Hill

Stained glass by J. H. Blaylock

The contour map of Fern Hill is seasonal
and topical heights and valleys—
you can almost rub your fingers
on its flat surface and feel the rise
and fall of earth's chest, relaxing.
This world is a coherence of opposites
meeting and repelling.
We need to find commonality
to negotiate our differences
passing through generations
like a bad inheritance.
Someone needs to realize the insanity of arguing
and expecting different outcomes. Surely, people
remember the calm days of their childhood
when problems never troubled their world,
and the sky stared back with mercy. Now,
children know no peace;
the sky falls on their heads.
Someone needs to talk about the madness.
Someone needs to point to another way,
like it was a map to reasonable thinking,
and say, *there it is.*

MARTIN WILLITTS, JR.

The Townspeople Thought I Knew the Weather

They all want to know if it is safe to hang the laundry,
or if the weather will hold for golf, or will the winds
be fair and wild as a new lover. But this is Swansea
where it rains whenever it is not raining. As I was a lad
till now when I do not know any better, I am drenched
and leak whenever I enter a room, waterlogged,
smelling of soaked leaves.

They ask me what the weather is like, looking out
at the drenching rain. It is always better to lie
about such things and smile as a fox caught with a chicken
than to tell the god awful truth—it is rain thick as carrots;
what else is new? Just give it a while or two.
The misery cannot keep up forever.
Every once in a while we catch a break.
If you live to be a hundred, you might see the skies open
and wonder what that blue stuff is.

I tell them to think of the small openings between showers,
the ones where we dodge quick as we can.
Those moments when familiarity
looks totally new again.

That never works, they tell me.
We take spoons of sunshine like it was bad medicine.
We hide when the day is swamped, dropping rain like tides.

Above the Spring Taff

Painting by Guy Manning

The steep hill towards the sun through the white pine
is where woodpeckers knock searching for insects.
In this spring where you can still feel young,
there is a different kind of silence when sounds
are more intense, where you can hear grass in wind
singing about the on-coming light rain,
where light itself rains between the drops
tapping on pine needles like tuning forks.

All the absence in your life is filled. There is no need to rush
through damp grass towards sunlight. It will be there
when you need it. Just listen to the katydid
and spring water after ice melt clears its throat.
Above the spring leaves, the stars are greening.
If we climb these hills, we might reach them before we die.

Opus 10

When I die, I want to leave behind
something more than I take with me.
Something close to a heartbeat of a hummingbird
with tiny, oscillating, gossamer wings
tasting poems of memory.
And in this instance, speak well of me.
Say, he had love and loved back, equally.

In the loud darkness, sing well!
Like dizzy winds against restless branches, sing!

Say, he did the best he could
under the circumstances,
and perhaps, although it was not enough,
he tried with his whole heart,
murmuring against a gale
across the lake of hopelessness.

For this is all I could do. Hoping
against hope, it was enough.

MARTIN WILLITTS, JR.

Living in a Four-Season Land

Days do not blend into wonder, but arrive
in fits and flurry, an unsettling of birds.

Leaves are budding, dreaming of leafing
and falling, and composting and coming back again.

I cannot get enough of these salt winds,
or leaves taking into skies like geese, or bleeding sun,

or dryness or drenching, or scattered shells on beaches,
or prickly things, or swelling lakes, or doors of night.

Persistence of Memory

(after the painting by Salvador Dali)

When I realized all the clocks had melted I knew
I was finally free, that I'd wander this barren land
without hunger or thirst and I would stay this age
forever. I knew that the sleeping fish was really dead
and that the ants would eventually find him. I would
only remember the happy times of my life which total
47 minutes, and I'd play those 47 minutes over in my head
while my favorite music played from a speaker inside a cloud,
just inches out of the picture.

CONTRIBUTOR NOTES

Jeffrey Alfier is winner of the 2014 Kithara Book Prize for his poetry collection, *Idyll for a Vanishing River* (Glass Lyre Press, 2013). He is also author of *The Wolf Yearling* (Silver Birch Press) and *The Storm Petrel—Poems of Ireland* (Grayson Books). His recent work has appeared in *Spoon River Poetry Review, Saranac Review* and *Tulane Review.*

Shawn Aveningo is a globally published, award-winning poet who can't stand the taste of coconut, eats pistachios daily and loves shoes...especially red ones! She believes poetry, especially when read aloud, is the perfect literary art form for today's fast-paced world due to its power to stir emotion in less than two minutes. Shawn's poetry has appeared in over 60 literary journals, anthologies and e-zines including *Tincture Journal, Pirene's Fountain, Boston Poetry, PoeticDiversity, Convergence, Poetry Now, Tule Review,* a n d *Haunted Waters Press Quarterly.* She's given birth on two continents, and her three adult children make her an extremely proud "mama bear." She shares the creative life, and business (thePoetryBox.com), with her best friend & soul-mate, and they have recently made Portland, Oregon their home.

Mary Jo Balistreri has two books of poetry, *Joy in the Morning* and *gathering the harvest* published by Bellowing Ark Press. Her chapbook, *Best Brothers,* has just been released by Tiger's Eye Press. She has six Pushcart nominations and two Best of the Net. Mary Jo enjoys public speaking and does as many readings as possible. She is a founding member of "Grace River Poets," an outreach for women's shelters, schools, and churches. Please visit her for more information at maryjobalistreripoet.com.

Ruth Bavetta's poems have been published in *Rattle, Nimrod, Tar River Review, North American Review, Spillway, Rhino, Poetry East,* and *Poetry New Zealand,* among others, and are included in several anthologies. She has published two books, *Fugitive Pigments* and *Embers on the Stairs.* Her third book, *No Longer at this Address,* will appear soon. She loves the light on November afternoons, the smell of the ocean, a warm back to curl against in bed. She hates pretense, fundamentalism and sauerkraut.

Brian Beatty grew up in Brazil, Indiana, but now lives in Minneapolis, Minnesota. His jokes, poems, and stories have appeared in numerous print and online publications, including *Alba, The Bark, Conduit, Elephant Journal, elimae, The Evergreen Review, Exquisite Corpse, Forklift Ohio, Gulf Coast, Hobart, McSweeney's, Opium, Paper Darts, Phoebe, Revolver, Seventeen, WalkerArt.org* and *The Writer.* Recordings of Brian's poems and stories have been featured in several public arts projects. He also performs as a storyteller.

Sandy Benitez is the founder and editor of Flutter Press and Poppy Road Review. Flutter Press chapbooks were recently added to The University at Buffalo's Poetry Collection. She's been nominated for the Pushcart Prize, Dzanc's Best of the Web, and Best of the Net. Sandy has authored one full-length collection of poetry, five poetry chapbooks, and has appeared in three anthologies. She resides in Southern California with her husband and their two children.

Nancy Bevilaqua's work has been published in or is forthcoming from *Tupelo Quarterly, Mad Hat Lit, Atticus Review, Apogee Journal, Menacing Hedge, Construction, The Otter, Houseboat,* and other journals. She is the author of *Holding Breath: A Memoir of AIDS' Wildfire Days.* "Alabastron" is part of her collection *Gospel of the Throwaway Daughter,* which was published in December of 2014. She lives in Florida with her son.

Byron Beynon lives in Swansea, Wales. His work has appeared in several publications, including *Agenda, Poetry Wales, Worcester Review* (USA), *London Magazine, Warwick Review* and *Cyphers* (Dublin). Recent collections include *The Sundial* (Flutter Press), *Nocturne in Blue* (Lapwing Publications) and *The Echoing Coastline* (Agenda Editions).

George Bishop's work has appeared in *Avalon Literary Review* and *Flare.* Forthcoming work will be featured in *Carolina Quarterly* and at Toadlilly Press, which will publish his latest chapbook, *Short Lives & Solitudes.* Bishop won the 2013 Peter Meinke Prize at YellowJacket Press for his sixth chapbook, *Following Myself Home.* He attended Rutgers University and lives and writes in Saint Cloud, Florida.

CL Bledsoe's most recent novel is *Man of Clay* and his most recent poetry collection is *Riceland.* He's been nominated for the Pushcart Prize 13 times, had two stories selected as Notable Stories by Story South's Million Writers Award and two others nominated, and has been nominated for Best of the Net twice. He's also had a flash story selected for the long list of Wigleaf's 50 Best Flash Stories award. He blogs at clbledsoe.blogspot.com and reviews regularly for several publications. Bledsoe lives with his daughter in Virginia.

A German-born UK national, **Rose Mary Boehm** lives and works in Lima, Peru. Author of two novels and a poetry collection, *TANGENTS,* published in 2011 in the UK, her poems have appeared or are forthcoming in a good two dozen US poetry reviews as well as some print anthologies, and Diane Lockward's *The Crafty Poet.* She won third place in in the 2009 Margaret Reid Poetry Contest for Traditional Verse (US), was a semi-finalist in the Naugatuck 2012/13 Contest, and has been a finalist in several GR contests, winning it in October 2014.

Ace Boggess is the author of two books of poetry: *The Prisoners* (Brick Road Poetry Press, 2014) and *The Beautiful Girl Whose Wish Was Not Fulfilled* (Highwire Press, 2003). His writing has appeared in *Harvard Review, Mid-American Review, Atlanta Review, RATTLE, River Styx, Southern Humanities Review* and many other journals. He currently resides in Charleston, West Virginia.

Jesse Breite's recent poetry has appeared in *Tar River Poetry, The Nashville Review,* and *Prairie Schooner.* He has been featured in *Town Creek Poetry* and *The Southern Poetry Anthology, Volume V: Georgia.* FutureCycle Press published his first chapbook, *The Knife Collector,* in 2013. Jesse lives with his wife, Emily, in Atlanta, Georgia, but he was raised in Little Rock, Arkansas, and considers it his home.

Richard Brobst was co-founder and served as co-editor of the poetry journal, *Albatross,* from 1985-1998. In 1998 his first chapbook, *Inherited Roles,* was published under the Duane Locke Chapbook Series (Anabiosis Press). He currently has four chapbooks published, along with a number of individual poems in a wide variety of journals, reviews and anthologies, including *Pembroke Magazine, The California Quarterly, The Kentucky Poetry Review,* and *Florida in Verse, An Anthology.* Richard has recently retired from teaching English and conducting workshops across the south. He now spends a lot of time feeding cats.

Jeff Burt lives in Santa Cruz County, California, and works in manufacturing. He has published in *Thrice Fiction, Mobius, Windfall, Burningwood,* and *Nature Writing.*

Jefferson Carter has lived in Tucson since 1953, where he volunteers for Sky Island Alliance, a locally based environmental organization. He has been a featured reader at the Tucson Poetry Festival (2007) and the Tucson Festival of Books (2009, 2012, 2013). His work has appeared in journals like *Carolina Quarterly, Shenandoah, Cream City Review, Barrow Street* and *New Poets of the American West.* His fourth chapbook, *Tough Love,* won the Riverstone Poetry Press award. Chax Press published *Sentimental Blue, My Kind of Animal,* and *Get Serious: New and Selected Poems* (named a Southwest Best Book in 2013 by the Tucson/Pima County Public Library).

R.T. Castleberry is an internationally published poet and social critic. He was a co-founder of the Flying Dutchman Writers Troupe, co-editor/publisher of the poetry magazine *Curbside Review,* an assistant editor for *Lily Poetry Review* and *Ardent.* A 2014 Pushcart Prize nominee, his work has appeared most recently in *Santa Fe Literary Review, Caveat Lector, Comstock Review, Green Mountains Review, The Alembic, Paterson Literary Review, Silk Road* and *Argestes.* He was a finalist for the 2008 Arts & Letters/Rumi Prize for Poetry. In 1999, his work was chosen for the Metro Downtown Transit Streets Project "Texts In Context." His chapbook, *Arriving At The Riverside,* was published by Finishing Line Press in January, 2010. An e-book, *Dialogue and Appetite,* was published by Right Hand Pointing in May, 2011.

Alan Catlin has been publishing for five decades in the small, the minuscule, the unknown and the well known, from *Wordsworth's Socks* to *The Literary Review,* and many places in between. His archival collection of small press publications is now part of the University of Buffalo Special Collection. His most recent full-length book of poetry is *Alien Nation,* a compilation of four thematically related chapbooks.

Chelsea Cefalu earned her M.Ed from Lehigh University. Her work has appeared or is forthcoming in *Flutter Poetry Journal, Poppy Road Review, Decades, Bird's Thumb,* and the *Inflectionist.* She lives in Pennsylvania with her husband and children.

Sherry Chandler is the author of *The Woodcarver's Wife* and *Weaving a New Eden.* Her poems and reviews have appeared in many periodicals and anthologies, including *Vine Leaves,* the *Dead Mule School of Southern Literature,* and *qarrtsiluni.*

David Chorlton came to Phoenix from Europe in 1978 with his wife Roberta, an Arizona native. He quickly became comfortable with the climate while adjusting to the New World took longer. Writing and reading poetry have helped immensely in that respect, as has exposure to the American small presses. Arizona's landscape and wildlife became increasingly important to him both as a source of pleasure and a measure of how vulnerable the natural world is. His poetry often grows out of experiencing the Southwest, and both city (Phoenix) and countryside surface in his book, *The Devil's Sonata,* from FutureCycle Press, which also published his *Selected Poems.*

Sara Clancy is a Philadelphia transplant to the Desert Southwest. Her poems have appeared, or are forthcoming in *The Linnet's Wings, Crab Creek Review, The Madison Review, Antiphon, Verse Wisconsin, Turtle Island Quarterly, VAYAVYA* and *Houseboat,* where she was a featured poet. She lives in Arizona with her husband, their dog, and a 23-year-old goldfish named Darryl.

Chloe N. Clark is an MFA candidate in Creative Writing & Environment. Her work has appeared such places as *Sleet, Booth, Rock & Sling, Menacing Hedge,* and more. For her mini-rants on baked goods, television shows, books, and magic, she can be followed on Twitter @PintsNCupcakes, or check out her blog "Pints and Cupcakes" for more of her writing.

Joan Colby has published widely in journals such as *Poetry, Atlanta Review, South Dakota Review, The Spoon River Poetry Review, New York Quarterly, the new renaissance, Grand Street, Epoch,* and *Prairie Schooner.* Awards include two Illinois Arts Council Literary Awards, Rhino Poetry Award, the *new renaissance* Award for Poetry, and an Illinois Arts Council Fellowship in Literature. She was a finalist in the GSU Poetry Contest (2007), Nimrod International Pablo Neruda Prize (2009, 2012), and received honorable mentions in the *North American Review*'s James Hearst Poetry Contest (2008, 2010). Former editor of *Illinois Racing News,* she lives on a small horse farm in Northern Illinois. She has published 14 books, including *The Lonely Hearts Killers, The Atrocity Book, Dead Horses,* her *Selected Poems* (2013 FutureCycle Poetry Book Prize winner), *The Wingback Chair,* and *Bittersweet. Ribcage* is forthcoming from Glass Lyre Press.

C. Cleo Creech is a North Carolina native, raised on a tobacco farm, who now lives in Atlanta, GA. His art/chapbooks include *Dendrochronology, Flying Monkeys,* and *Phoenix Feathers.* He has been published in a number of journals and anthologies. He edited the acclaimed anthology, *Outside the Green Zone.* His piece, "The Peace of Gentle Waves," was recently turned into a major choral work.

Jim Davis is an MFA candidate at Northwestern University. His work has appeared in *Wisconsin Review, Seneca Review, Adirondack Review, Midwest Quarterly,* a n d *Contemporary American Voices,* among many others. Jim lives, writes, and paints in Chicago, where he reads for *TriQuarterly* and edits *North Chicago Review.*

Michael Diebert is the author of the collection *Life Outside the Set* (Sweatshoppe, 2013) and serves as poetry editor for *The Chattahoochee Review.* Other recent work has appeared in *Iodine Poetry Journal* and *jmww.* He teaches writing and literature at Georgia Perimeter College in Atlanta, where he also co-facilitates the Writers' Forum, a writing critique and feedback group.

donnarkevic, Weston, WV, has an MFA from National University. Recent poetry has appeared in *Bijou Poetry Review, Naugatuck River Review, Prime Number,* and *Off the Coast.* Poetry Chapbooks include *Laundry,* published by Main Street Rag. Plays have received readings in Chicago, New York, and Virginia. FutureCycle Press published *Admissions,* a book of poems, in 2013.

William Doreski lives in Peterborough, New Hampshire, and teaches at Keene State College. His most recent book of poetry is *The Suburbs of Atlantis* (2013). He has published three critical studies, including Robert Lowell's Shifting Colors. His essays, poetry, fiction, and reviews have appeared in many journals.

Robert Eastwood is a retired teacher who lives in San Ramon, California. He is a graduate of California State University At Los Angeles and Saint Mary's College. His work has appeared widely and most recently in *The Dirty Napkin, Wild Goose Poetry Review, Full Of Crow, Legendary, Softblow, Up The Staircase Quarterly, Literary Yard,* and *Loch Raven Review.* His chapbooks are *The Welkin Gate, Over Plainsong, Night of the Moth,* published by Small Poetry Press. He has been nominated twice for the Pushcart Prize.

Richard Fein was a finalist in The 2004 New York Center for Book Arts Chapbook Competition. A chapbook of his poems was published by Parallel Press, University of Wisconsin, Madison. He has published in many web and print journals, such as *Cordite, Cortland Review, Reed, Southern Review, Roanoke Review, Birmingham Poetry Review, Mississippi Review, Paris/atlantic, Canadian Dimension, Black Swan Review, Exquisite Corpse, Foliate Oak, Morpo Review, Ken*Again Oregon East, Southern Humanities Review, Morpo, Skyline, Touchstone, Windsor Review, Maverick, Parnassus Literary Review, Small Pond, Kansas Quarterly, Blue Unicorn, Exquisite Corpse, Terrain Aroostook Review, Compass Rose, Whiskey Island Review, Oregon East, Bad Penny Review, Constellations,* and many others.

William Ford has published two books of poems, *The Graveyard Picnic* (Mid-America Press, 2002) and *Past Present Imperfect* (Turning Point, 2006), and four chapbooks (two from Pudding House). Most recently his work has appeared in *Brilliant Corners, Hamilton Stone Review, The Hollins Critic, Lascaux Review, Monarch Review, Nashville Review, Southern Humanities Review, Valparaiso Poetry Review, Verse Wisconsin, The Wallace Stevens Journal,* and elsewhere. A retired teacher and editor, Ford lives in Iowa City, Iowa.

Joshua Gage is an ornery curmudgeon from Cleveland. His first full-length collection, *breaths,* is available from VanZeno Press. *Intrinsic Night,* a collaborative project he wrote with J. E. Stanley, was published by Sam's Dot Publishing. His most recent collection, *Inhuman: Haiku from the Zombie Apocalypse,* is available on Poet's Haven Press. He is a graduate of the Low Residency MFA Program in Creative Writing at Naropa University. He has a penchant for Pendleton shirts, rye whiskey, and any poem strong enough to yank the breath out of his lungs.

Bill Glose is a former paratrooper, Gulf War veteran, and author of the poetry collections *Half a Man* (FutureCycle Press, 2013) and *The Human Touch* (San Francisco Bay Press, 2007). In 2011, he was named the Daily Press Poet Laureate. His poems have appeared in numerous publications, including *Narrative Magazine, Poet Lore,* and *Southern California Review.* Now a full-time writer, he undertakes intriguing pursuits—such as walking across Virginia and participating in a world-record-setting skinny dip event—and writes about them for magazines. His website (www.BillGlose.com) includes a page of helpful information for writers.

James Grabill's poems have appeared in numerous periodicals such as *Stand* (UK), *Magma* (UK), *Toronto Quarterly* (CAN), *Harvard Review* (US), *Terrain* (US), *Seneca Review* (US), *Urthona* (UK), *kayak* (US), *Plumwood Mountain* (AUS), *Caliban* (US), *Mobius* (US), *Spittoon* (US), *Weber: The Contemporary West* (US), *The Common Review* (US), and *Buddhist Poetry Review* (US). Wordcraft of Oregon has published his new project of environmental prose poems, *Sea-Level Nerve: Book One* in 2014, with *Book Two* scheduled for 2015. A long-time Oregon resident, he teaches "systems thinking" relative to sustainability.

M. Krockmalnik Grabois' poems have appeared in hundreds of literary magazines in the U.S. and abroad. He is a regular contributor to *The Prague Revue* and has been nominated for the Pushcart Prize, most recently for his story "Purple Heart" published in *The Examined Life* in 2012, and for his poem. "Birds," published in *The Blue Hour,* 2013. His novel, *Two-Headed Dog,* based on his work as a clinical psychologist in a state hospital, is available for 99 cents from Kindle and Nook, or as a print edition.

Lori Gravley writes poetry, fiction, and creative nonfiction. She earned her MFA from the University of Texas at El Paso. She has published poems and essays in a variety of journals, including *Flights, Nebo,* and the *Rio Grande Review.* She has poems forthcoming in *Ekphrasis* and *Mock Turtle Zine.* She lives just outside of Yellow Springs, Ohio between a meadow and a cornfield.

William Greenway's *Selected Poems* won the 2014 FutureCycle Poetry Book Prize. Both his tenth and eleventh collections won Ohio Poetry Book of the Year Awards. He has published in *Poetry, American Poetry Review, Georgia Review, Southern Review, Poetry Northwest, Shenandoah,* and *Prairie Schooner.* He is Distinguished Professor of English at Youngstown State University.

Pat Hanahoe-Dosch has an MFA from the University of Arizona in Tucson, Arizona, and is currently an Associate Professor of English at Harrisburg Area Community College, Lancaster campus. Her poems have been published in *The Atticus Review, Confrontation, The Red River Review, San Pedro River Review, Red Ochre Lit, Nervous Breakdown, Quantum Poetry Magazine, The Paterson Literary Review, Abalone Moon, Switched-on Gutenberg, Malala: Poems for Malala Yousafzai* (a Good Works anthology to raise money for the Malala Fund), and *Paterson: The Poets' City* (an anthology edited by Maria Mazziotti Gillan), among others. Her articles have appeared in *Travel Belles, On a Junket,* and *Wholistic Living News.* Her flash fiction story, "Serendip," was published in the *In Posse Review,* #31. Her story, "Sighting Bia," was selected as a finalist for A Room of Her Own Foundation's Orlando Prize for Flash Fiction. FutureCycle Press published her book, *Fleeing Back.*

Sarah Hina hails from Athens, Ohio. Her work's been published in *The Lascaux Review,* and her debut novel, *Plum Blossoms in Paris,* is available from Medallion Press.

Katherine Hoerth is the author of two poetry collections, *Goddess Wears Cowboy Boots* (Lamar University Press, 2014) and *The Garden Uprooted* (Slough Press, 2012). She teaches literature and creative writing at the University of Texas Pan American and serves as the poetry editor of *Amarillo Bay.* Her work has been included in journals such as *Pleiades, Front Porch,* and *Hawai'i Pacific Review.* She lives in deep south Texas with her love, Bruno, and their pride of lazy house cats.

Karen Paul Holmes is the author of a full-length poetry collection, *Untying the Knot* (Aldrich Press, 2014). Her poetry has appeared in publications such as *Atlanta Review, POEM, The Sow's Ear Poetry Review, American Society: What Poets See* (FutureCycle Press), and *The Southern Poetry Anthology Vol 5: Georgia* (Texas Review Press).

Paul Hostovsky is the author of five books of poetry and six poetry chapbooks. His *Selected Poems* was published by FutureCycle Press in 2014. His poems have won a Pushcart Prize, two Best of the Net awards, and have been featured on *Poetry Daily, Verse Daily,* and *The Writer's Almanac.* He was a Featured Poet on the 2013 Georgia Poetry Circuit. He makes his living in Boston as an interpreter for the Deaf.

A. J. Huffman has published seven solo chapbooks and one joint chapbook through various small presses. Her eighth solo chapbook, *Drippings from a Painted Mind,* won the 2013 Two Wolves Chapbook Contest. She is a Pushcart Prize nominee, and her poetry, fiction, haiku, and photography have appeared in hundreds of national and international journals, including *Labletter, The James Dickey Review, Bone Orchard, EgoPHobia, Kritya,* and *Offerta Speciale,* in which her work appeared in both English and Italian translation. She is also the founding editor of Kind of a Hurricane Press. www.kindofahurricanepress.com.

Henry Hughes' poems have appeared in *Antioch Review, Carolina Quarterly, Shenandoah, Southern Humanities Review, Seattle Review,* and *Poetry Northwest.* He is the author of three poetry collections, including *Men Holding Eggs,* which received the 2004 Oregon Book Award. Hughes also edited the *Everyman's Library* anthologies, *The Art of Angling: Poems about Fishing* and *Fishing Stories.* His commentary on new poetry appears regularly in *Harvard Review.*

Joseph Hutchison is the author of 15 collections of poems, including *Marked Men, Thread of the Real, The Earth-Boat,* and *Bed of Coals* (winner of the 1994 Colorado Poetry Award). He makes his living as a commercial writer and as an adjunct professor of graduate level writing and literature at the University of Denver's University College. He and his wife, yoga instructor Melody Madonna, live in the mountains southwest of Denver.

M. J. Iuppa lives on a small farm near the shores of Lake Ontario. Her most recent poems have appeared in *Poetry East, The Chariton Review, Tar River Poetry, Blueline, The Prose Poem Project,* and *The Centrifugal Eye,* among other publications. Her most recent poetry chapbook is *As the Crow Flies* (Foothills Publishing, 2008), and her second full-length collection is *Within Reach* (Cherry Grove Collections, 2010). *Between Worlds,* a prose chapbook, was published by Foothills Publishing in May 2013. She is Writer-in-Residence and Director of the Visual and Performing Arts Minor program at St. John Fisher College in Rochester, New York.

Mike James has been widely published in magazines throughout the country and is the author of seven poetry collections. His two most recent collections are *Elegy in Reverse* (2014, Aldrich Press) and *Past Due Notices: Poems 1991-2011* (2012, Main Street Rag.) He lives just outside of Atlanta, Georgia with his wife and children.

Carole Johnston, poet and novelist, taught creative writing at the School for Creative and Performing Arts in Lexington, Kentucky, for eighteen years. Now retired, she drives around Bluegrass backroads with a notebook and camera, capturing those "zen moments." She has published poems in numerous journals, and her poetry collection, *Journeys: Getting Lost,* will be published in 2015 by Finishing Line Press.

Laura M. Kaminski grew up in northern Nigeria, went to school in New Orleans, and currently lives in rural Missouri. Her poems have recently appeared in *The Lake, One Sentence Poems,* and elsewhere. Several of her poems archived at The Poetry Storehouse have been used as the basis for video-poems during 2014. She is an Associate Editor at *Right Hand Pointing.*

Collin Kelley is the author of the novels *Conquering Venus* and *Remain In Light,* which have just been re-issued in new editions by Sibling Rivalry Press. His poetry collections include *Better To Travel, Slow To Burn, After the Poison,* and *Render,* chosen by the American Library Association for its 2014 Over the Rainbow Book List. A recipient of the Georgia Author of the Year Award, Deep South Festival of Writers Award and Goodreads Poetry Award, Kelley's poetry, essays and interviews have appeared in magazines, journals and anthologies around the world. He is currently writing his third novel, *Leaving Paris.*

Clyde Kessler lives in Radford, Virginia, with his wife Kendall (an artist and photographer) and their son Alan. They have an art studio called Towhee Hill in their home. He is a member of Blue Ridge Discovery Center, an environmental education organization with programs in western North Carolina and southwestern Virginia. He is also a regional editor for *Virginia Birds,* a publication of the Virginia Society of Ornithology. He has published poems in many magazines, recently in *Decades Review, Still, Leaves of Ink, San Pedro River Review, Belle Rêve,* and *Town Creek Review.* His book, *Fiddling at Midnight's Farmhouse,* will be published in 2016 by Cedar Creek Publishing.

Philip Kobylarz is a teacher and writer of fiction, poetry, book reviews, and essays. He has worked as a journalist and film critic for newspapers in Memphis, TN. His work appears in such publications as *Paris Review, Poetry,* and *The Best American Poetry* series. The author of a book of poems concerning life in the south of France, he has a collection of short fiction and a book-length essay forthcoming.

Jennifer Lagier has published nine books of poetry and in a variety of literary magazines. She was nominated for a Pushcart in 2011, taught with California Poets in the Schools and is now a retired college librarian/instructor, member of the Italian American Writers Association, Pacific Northwest Writers Association, Rockford Writers Guild, co-edits the *Homestead Review* and *The Monterey Poetry Review,* maintains websites for *Ping Pong: A Literary Journal of the Henry Miller Library* a n d *misfitmagazine.net.* She also helps coordinate the Monterrey Bay Poetry Consortium's Second Sunday Reading Series. Visit her website at jlagier.net.

Marie Lecrivain is the editor-publisher of *poeticdiversity: the litzine of Los Angeles,* a photographer, and a writer-in-residence at her apartment. She's received two 2014 Pushcart nominations, and her work has appeared in various journals, including *Edgar Allen Poet Journal, Maitenant, Kentucky Review, A New Ulster, Paper Nautilus, The Los Angeles Review, Poetry Salzburg Review,* and others. She's the author of *The Virtual Tablet of Irma Tre* (Edgar & Lenore's Publishing House, 2014) and the forthcoming *Grimm Conversations* (Sybaritic Press, 2015). She's the editor of the upcoming anthology, *Rubicon: Words and Art Inspired by Oscar Wilde's De Profundis* (Sybaritic Press, 2015). Her avocations include alchemy, making jewelry, H.P. Lovecraft, Vincent Price, steampunk accessories, and the letter "S."

Helen Losse is the author of three books of poetry: *Facing a Lonely West*, just released from Main Street Rag, *Seriously Dangerous,* and *Better With Friends,* as well as three chapbooks. Her poems have been included in various anthologies, including *Literary Trails of the North Carolina Piedmont,* forthcoming in *The Southern Poetry Anthology, Volume VII: North Carolina,* nominated twice for a Pushcart Prize, and three times for a Best of the Net award, one of which was a finalist. A former Poetry Editor for *The Dead Mule School of Southern Literature,* she is now an Associate Editor for *Kentucky Review.*

Bruce McCandless is a writer and editor who lives in Austin, Texas with his wife and two daughters. His stories and poems have appeared in a number of journals, including *Pleiades, Borderlands, Cold Mountain Review, New Delta Review,* and *The Seattle Review.* He is also the author of the novels *Sour Lake,* published in 2011, and *Cyrenaica,* which will appear in early 2015.

Jennifer A. McGowan obtained her MA and PhD from the University of Wales. Despite being certified as disabled at age 16 with Ehlers-Danlos Syndrome, she has persevered and has published poetry and prose in many magazines and anthologies on both sides of the Atlantic. She won the Geoff Stevens Memorial Prize 2014, as a result of which her first full-length collection, *The Weight of Coming Home,* will be published in 2015 by Indigo Dreams Publishing. She has also been Highly Commended in the prestigious Torbay Poetry Competition and the Manchester Cathedral Poetry Competition. *Life in Captivity* and *Sounding,* her pamphlets, are available through Finishing Line Press. Her website, with more poetry and examples of her mediaeval calligraphy, can be found at www.jenniferamcgowan.com and handwritten versions of her poems can be purchased at www.handwrittenpoems.co.uk.

Pushcart-nominee **Bruce McRae** is a Canadian musician with over 900 publications, including *Poetry.com* and *The North American Review.* His first book, *The So-Called Sonnets,* is available from the Silenced Press website or via Amazon books. To hear his music and view more poems visit "BruceMcRaePoetry" on Youtube.

Jacqueline Markowski's work has most recently appeared in *San Pedro River Review, The Doctor TJ Eckleburg Review, Bird's Thumb, Rust+Moth, S/tick, Emerge Literary Journal* and is forthcoming in *Up the Staircase Quarterly, The Knicknackery, Barely South Review* and *Turtle Island Quarterly.* A multiple Pushcart nominee, she won first place at The Sandhills Writer's Conference and was a semi-finalist for the 2014 Auburn Witness Poetry Prize. She is currently working on a collection of poetry. You can see more of her work at jacquelinemarkowski.com.

Todd Mercer of Grand Rapids, Michigan won the first Woodstock Writers Festival's Flash Fiction contest. His chapbook, *Box of Echoes,* won the Michigan Writers Cooperative Press contest and his digital chapbook, *Life-wish Maintenance,* is forthcoming from RHP Books. Mercer's poetry and fiction appear in *Apocrypha & Abstractions, The Bactrian Room, Blink Ink, Blue Collar Review, The Camel Saloon, Camroc Press Review, Cease, Cows, Cheap Pop, Dunes Review, East Coast Literary Review, Eunoia Review, Falling Star, 50-Word Stories, The Fib Review, Gravel, The Lake, The Legendary, Main Street Rag Anthologies, Melancholy Hyperbole, Misty Mountain Review, Mobius: The Journal of Social Change, theNewer York, One Sentence Poems, Postcard Poems and Prose, Postcard Shorts, Right Hand Pointing, River Lit, The Second Hump,* and *Spartan.*

Scott Minar is the author of *The Body's Fire* (Clarellen 2002) and *The Palace of Reasons* (Mammoth Books 2006); coauthor (with Edward Dougherty) of *Exercises for Poets: Double Bloom* (Pearson/Prentice Hall 2006); and editor of *The Working Poet: 75 Writing Exercises and a Poetry Anthology* (Autumn House 2009) and *The Working Poet II: 50 Writing Exercises and a Poetry Anthology* (Mammoth Books 2014). His poems have appeared in *The Paris Review, Poetry International, Crazyhorse, The Georgia Review, Ninth Letter, TickleAce, West Branch, The Laurel Review, Verse Daily,* and other journals and anthologies in the U.S. and Canada. His third full-length poetry collection is titled *Cymbalism* and will be available from Mammoth Books in 2015. He is currently Professor of English at Ohio University Lancaster.

Anderson O'Brien lives in Columbia, SC with her husband and two dogs. She has published poetry in *Iodine Poetry Journal, Blue Fifth Review, Red River Review, The Dead Mule of Southern Literature, Heavy Bear,* and *Flutter.*

Anne Britting Oleson has been published widely in North America, Europe and Asia. She earned her MFA at the Stonecoast program of USM. She has published two chapbooks, *The Church of St. Materiana* (Moon Pie Press, 2007) and *The Beauty of It* (Sheltering Pines Press, 2010); a third, *Planes and Trains and Automobiles,* is forthcoming in spring of 2015 from Portent Press.

Shawnte Orion's first book of poetry, *The Existentialist Cookbook,* was published by NYQBooks. His poems have appeared in *The Threepenny Review, Barrelhouse, Gargoyle Magazine,* and *Crab Creek Review.* He has been invited to read at bookstores, bars, universities, hair salons, museums, and laundromats. She blogs at batteredhive.blogspot.com.

Two books of **James Owens**'s poems have been published: *An Hour is the Doorway* (Black Lawrence Press) and *Frost Lights a Thin Flame* (Mayapple Press). His poems, reviews, translations, and photographs have appeared widely in literary journals, including recent or upcoming publications in *Poppy Road Review, The Stinging Fly, The Cresset,* and *Valparaiso Poetry Review.* He has an MFA from the University of Alabama and lives in central Indiana and northern Ontario.

Originally from Greenwood, SC, **Scott Owens** holds degrees from Ohio University, UNC Charlotte, and UNC Greensboro. He currently lives in Hickory, NC, where he teaches at Catawba Valley Community College, edits *Wild Goose Poetry Review* and serves as vice-president of the NC Poetry Society. His 11th book of poetry, *Eye of the Beholder,* was recently released by Main Street Rag. His work has received awards from the Academy of American Poets, the Pushcart Prize Anthology, the Next Generation/Indie Lit Awards, the NC Writers Network, the NC Poetry Society, and the Poetry Society of SC.

William Page's third collection of poems, *Bodies Not Our Own* (Memphis State University Press), was awarded a Walter R. Smith Distinguished Book Award. *William Page's Greatest Hits: 1970-2000* is from Pudding House Publications. His poems have appeared in such journals as *The Southern Review, Sewanee Review, North American Review, Southwest Review, Rattle, Ploughshares, Literary Review, American Literary Review, Southern Poetry Review, Valparaiso Poetry Review, The Midwest Quarterly, Pedestal Magazine, North Dakota Quarterly, Wisconsin Review, South Carolina Review,* and in numerous anthologies, most recently in *The Southern Poetry Anthology Volume VI: Tennessee.* He is founding editor of *The Pinch*.

Jimmy Pappas holds an MA in English Literature from Rivier University. After serving in the Air Force training soldiers in Vietnam, he taught high school English, poetry, and philosophy until his recent retirement. He is a frequent reader at poetry events around the state of New Hampshire and facilitates writing workshops for adults and young poets. Jimmy is currently preparing four collections of his work for publication. His poems have been published in such journals as *Atticus Review, Red River Review, Poppy Road Review, Apeiron Review, The Poets' Touchstone* and *War, Literature and the Arts.* In 2014 he won first prize in the Poetry Society of New Hampshire's National Contest.

Lee Passarella acts as senior literary editor for *Atlanta Review* magazine and served as editor-in-chief of Coreopsis Books, a poetry-book publisher. He also writes classical music reviews for *Audiophile Audition.* Passarella's poetry has appeared in *Chelsea, Cream City Review, Louisville Review, The Formalist, Antietam Review, Journal of the American Medical Association, The Literary Review, Edge City Review, The Wallace Stevens Journal, Snake Nation Review, Umbrella, Slant, Cortland Review,* and many other periodicals and ezines. *Swallowed up in Victory,* Passarella's long narrative poem based on the American Civil War, was published by White Mane Books in 2002. It has been praised by poet Andrew Hudgins as a work that is "compelling and engrossing as a novel." Passarella has published two full-length poetry collections: *The Geometry of Loneliness* (David Robert Books, 2006) and *Redemption* (FutureCycle Press, 2014). His chapbook is *Sight-Reading Schumann* (Pudding House Publications, 2007).

Tim Peeler's latest book is *Rough Beast* from FutureCycle Press. In addition to four books on local and regional baseball history, he has published five other books of poetry. His work has appeared in numerous magazines and journals and has been included in anthologies from Time/Life, Simon & Schuster, and in an HBO documentary.

Frederick Pollack is author of two book-length narrative poems, *The Adventure* and *Happiness,* both published by Story Line Press. A collection of shorter poems, *A Poverty of Words,* is forthcoming in 2015 from Prolific Press. Pollack has appeared in *Hudson Review, Salmagundi, Poetry Salzburg Review, Die Gazette* (Munich), *The Fish Anthology* (Ireland), *Representations, Magma* (UK), *Bateau, Fulcrum, Chiron Review, Chicago Quarterly Review,* etc. Online, poems have appeared in *Big Bridge, Hamilton Stone Review, Diagram, BlazeVox, The New Hampshire Review, Mudlark,* etc. Recent Web publications in *Occupoetry, Faircloth Review, Camel Saloon, Kalkion, Gap Toothed Madness.* Adjunct professor of creative writing at George Washington University. Poetics: neither navel-gazing mainstream nor academic pseudo-avant-garde.

Connie Post served as Poet Laureate of Livermore, California (2005 to 2009). Her work has appeared in *Calyx, Kalliope, The Big Muddy, Cold Mountain Review, Crab Creek Review, Comstock Review, Slipstream, Spoon River Poetry Review,* and *Valparaiso Poetry Review.* She won the 2009 Caesura Poetry Award. She has been short listed for the *Calyx* Lois Cranston Memorial Award, the *I 70 Review* award, and the *Comstock Review* Muriel Craft Bailey Awards. Her chapbook *And When the Sun Drops* won the Aurorean Fall 2012 Editor's Choice award. Her first full-length book, *FloodWater* (Glass Lyre Press, 2014), won the 2014 Lyrebird Award.

Stephen Roger Powers started writing poetry thirteen years ago to pass time in the middle of the night when he was too energized to sleep after coming off the stage in comedy clubs around the Midwest. He is the author of *The Follower's Tale* and *Hello, Stephen,* both published by Salmon Poetry. He hasn't done stand-up in a long time, but every once in a while he finds avenues for the performer he was born to be. He was an extra in *Joyful Noise* with Queen Latifah and Dolly Parton, and he can be seen if you know just where to look.

Ken Poyner often serves as unlikely eye-candy at his wife's powerlifting meets. His latest collection of brief, quizzical fictions, *Constant Animals,* can be located through links on his website, www.kpoyner.com, also at www.amazon.com, and at a number of impressionable bookstores. He has had recent work out in *Analog, Asimov's, Poet Lore, Sein und Werden, Cream City Review, Menacing Hedge,* and a few dozen other places. He and his wife strive to be responsible cat and fish parents.

David Radavich's recent poetry collections are *America Bound: An Epic for Our Time* (2007), *Canonicals: Love's Hours* (2009), and *Middle-East Mezze* (2011). His plays have been produced across the U.S., including six Off-Off-Broadway, and in Europe. He has performed in a variety of countries and served as president of the Thomas Wolfe Society, Charlotte Writers' Club, and other groups. His latest book is *The Countries We Live In* (2014). See www.davidradavich.org.

JC Reilly is author of the chapbook, *La Petite Mort* (Finishing Line Press), and 25% co-author of a recently released anthology of occasional verse, *On Occasion: Four Poets, One Year,* from Poetry Atlanta Press. She has had work published in *The Louisville Review, Southern Women's Review, Xavier Review, Cider Press Review, and Java Monkey Speaks Anthology IV,* among others. She lives in Atlanta with her three cats, a husband, and possibly a ghost. The two poems published here are from a narrative collection (a "poenovella") about twin sisters living in Shreveport, Louisiana (the author's hometown) in the early part of the 20th Century. The sisters, Tallulah and Vidalia, are actually descended from a line of herbalist witches, although their more "magickal" side does not show up so much in these poems. These focus on Vi's stay at the Highland Sanitarium, where Vi was committed after she was raped by the book's antagonist.

Jonathan K. Rice is founding editor and publisher of *Iodine Poetry Journal,* which is in its fifteenth year of publication and is distinguished by having work included in *Best American Poetry 2006.* Jonathan is the author of a chapbook, *Shooting Pool With A Cellist* (Main Street Rag, 2003) and a full-length collection, *Ukulele and Other Poems* (Main Street Rag, 2006). His poetry has appeared in numerous publications, and he has been a longtime host of poetry readings in Charlotte, NC, where he lives with his family. In 2012 he received the Irene Blair Honeycutt Legacy Award for outstanding service in support of local and regional writers, awarded by Central Piedmont Community College. He is also a visual artist.

P. R. Rice is a part-time writer, part-time therapist, and full time writerpist in Seattle, Washington. His work has previously been published in *The Minetta Review, Poetry Quarterly,* and *Paper Nautilus.*

Mary Ricketson, Murphy, NC, has been writing for 20 years to satisfy a hunger. She is inspired by nature and her work as a counselor. Her poetry has been published in *Wild Goose Poetry Review, FutureCycle, Journal of Kentucky Studies, Lights in the Mountains, Echoes Across the Blue Ridge* and *Freeing Jonah.* She has published a chapbook, *I Hear the River Call My Name,* and a full-length collection, *Hanging Dog Creek.* She is a member of North Carolina Writers Network, North Carolina Poetry Society, and is president of Ridgeline Literary Alliance.

Katherine Riegel is the author of two books of poetry, *What the Mouth Was Made For* and *Castaway.* Her poems and essays have appeared in a variety of journals, including *Brevity, Crazyhorse,* and *The Rumpus.* She is co-founder and poetry editor for *Sweet: A Literary Confection.* Visit her at katherineriegel.com.

Ron Riekki's books include *U.P.* (nominated for the Great Michigan Read and by John Casey for the Sewanee Writers Series) and *The Way North: Collected Upper Peninsula New Works,* a 2014 Michigan Notable Book, 2014 Midwest Book Award finalist, Foreword Book of the Year Award finalist, 2014 Next Generation Indie Book Award finalist, and 2014 Eric Hoffer Book Award finalist (shortlisted for the Grand Prize), wsupress.wayne.edu/books/detail/way-north.

Peg Robarchek is a published novelist and poet living in Charlotte, North Carolina. Her first collection of poetry, *Inventing Sex,* will be published by Main Street Rag in early 2015. Recent acceptances also include *Naugatuck River Review, Prime Number, Blast Furnace, Red Earth Review, Iodine Poetry Journal,* and *Kakalak 2014.*

Susan Rooke has recent or forthcoming poems in *Concho River Review, Naugatuck River Review, Red Weather, Texas Poetry Calendar 2015,* and the anthology *Pushing the Envelope: Epistolary Poems* (ed. Jonas Zdanys, Lamar University Press). A three-time Pushcart Prize nominee and Best of the Net nominee, she hopes to publish her fantasy novel, *The Space Between,* in the coming year. She lives in Austin, Texas.

Don Schofield's poems, essays and translations have appeared in numerous American and international journals. A recipient of the 2010 Criticos Prize (UK), he has also received honors from, among others, the State University of New York, Anhinga Press, Southern California Anthology and Princeton University, where he was a Stanley J. Seeger Writer-in-Residence. His poetry volumes include *Of Dust* (March Street Press, 1991); *Approximately Paradise* (University Press of Florida, 2002); *Kindled Terraces: American Poets in Greece* (Truman State University Press, 2004); *The Known: Selected Poems (of Nikos Fokas), 1981-2000* (Ypsilon Books, 2010) and *Before Kodachrome* (FutureCycle Press, 2012). A resident of Greece for many years, he is currently the Dean of Special Programs at Perrotis College, a division of the American Farm School.

Judith Skillman's work has appeared in *Poetry, Prairie Schooner, FIELD, Seneca Review, The Iowa Review, Southern Review,* and other journals. Skillman is the recipient of grants from the Academy of American Poets, Washington State Arts Commission, and King County Arts Commission. She teaches at Richard Hugo House in Seattle, Washington. Her new book *House of Burnt Offerings* is forthcoming from Tebot Bach Press. Visit judithskillman.com.

Eric Steineger teaches English in Western North Carolina. He is the Senior Poetry Editor of *The Citron Review,* while his work has been featured in such places as *The Los Angeles Review, Elimae,* and *Tinderbox.* Recent influences on his work include domestic life in Asheville, Fernando Pessoa, and collaborations with poets and musicians.

Tim Suermondt is the author of two full-length collections: *Trying to Help the Elephant Man Dance* (The Backwaters Press, 2007) and *Just Beautiful* (New York Quarterly Books, 2010). He has published poems in *Poetry, The Georgia Review, Blackbird, Able Muse, Prairie Schooner, PANK, Bellevue Literary Review, Stand Magazine* (U.K.), and has poems forthcoming in *december magazine, Plume Poetry Journal, North Dakota Quarterly,* among others. After many years in Queens and Brooklyn, he has moved to Cambridge with his wife, the poet Pui Ying Wong.

Victoria Sullivan is a young writer of poetry and prose from Vanceburg, Kentucky. She is a recent graduate of Transylvania University and plans to pursue her Master's degree in English at the University of Kentucky. Her work has been published in *Still: The Journal* and *The Transylvanian,* Transylvania University's arts journal.

Alice Teeter studied poetry at Eckerd College with Peter Meinke. Her chapbook *20 CLASS A* was published in 1975 by Morningstar Media, Tallahassee, Florida. Her collection of poems *String Theory* won the Georgia Poetry Society's 2008 Charles B. Dickson Chapbook Contest, judged by poet Lewis Turco, and her book *When It Happens To You...* was published in 2009 by Star Cloud Press. Her latest collection, *Elephant Girls,* will be published by Aldrich Press in August 2015. She served as an Adjunct Professor, Lecturer in Poetry, at Emory University in Atlanta, Georgia, from 2011 through 2013.

Alarie Tennille was born and raised in Portsmouth, Virginia, and graduated from the University of Virginia in the first class admitting women. She misses the ocean but loves the writing community she's found in Kansas City. Alarie serves on the Emeritus Board of The Writers Place. She's the author of a new poetry collection, *Running Counterclockwise* (2014) and a chapbook, *Spiraling into Control* (2010). Alarie's poems have appeared in numerous journals, including *Margie, Poetry East, Coal City Review, English Journal, Wild Goose Poetry Review,* and *Southern Women's Review.* Please visit her new website at alariepoet.com.

Aden Thomas lives in Laramie, Wyoming. His work has previously appeared in *Common Ground Review, Dressing Room Poetry Journal, Third Wednesday,* and *The San Pedro River Review.*

Allison Thorpe is new to Lexington after decades of living among the whippoorwills and wilds of Kentucky. She is the author of *Thoughts While Swinging a Wild Child in a Green Mesh Hammock* (Janze Publications), *Swooning and Other Art Forms* (a NFSPS chapbook winner), *What She Sees: Poems for Georgia O'Keefe* (forthcoming from White Knuckle Press), and *To This Sad and Lovely Land* (runner-up in 2014 Gambling the Aisle Chapbook Contest). Recent work appears or is forthcoming in *South85 Journal, Scapegoat Review, The Meadow, The Citron Review, Front Range Review, The Heartland Review, Agave Magazine, Naugatuck River Review,* and *Motif v4—seeking its own level: an anthology of writings about water,* among others. A Pushcart nominee, she is currently working on her first novel.

After many years of educational administration and teaching college students the art of communication, **Jill White** entered her "second life," tapping into her creative self as a poet and award-winning jewelry artist. You can read some of her more recent poetry in *The Olentangy Review, The Cumberland River Review, U.S.1 Worksheets,* and *The Dead Mule School of Southern Literature,* and you can see her jewelry at art festivals throughout the Southeast. When not at the writing desk or jewelry bench, she can be found with her nose in a book on her porch overlooking the bayou.

Dana Wildsmith's blog, *Jumping: A journey through the writing of a novel,* documents the process of writing a novel based on immigration stories and border issues. Her environmental memoir, *Back to Abnormal: Surviving With An Old Farm in the New South,* was Finalist for Georgia Author of the Year. She is the author of five collections of poetry, including most recently, *Christmas in Bethlehem.* Wildsmith has served as Artist-in-Residence for Grand Canyon National Park, as Writer-in-Residence for the Island Institute in Sitka, Alaska, and she is a Fellow of the Hanbidge Center for Creative Arts and Sciences. Wildsmith teaches English Literacy through Lanier Technical College.

John Sibley Williams is the author of eight collections, most recently *Controlled Hallucinations* (FutureCycle Press, 2013). He is the winner of the HEART Poetry Award and has been nominated for the Pushcart, Rumi, and The Pinch Poetry Prizes. John serves as editor of *The Inflectionist Review* and Board Member of the Friends of William Stafford. A few previous publishing credits include *American Literary Review, Third Coast, Nimrod International Journal, Rio Grande Review, Inkwell, Cider Press Review, Bryant Literary Review, Cream City Review, RHINO,* and various anthologies. He lives in Portland, OR.

Martin Willitts, Jr. has 28 chapbooks including national chapbook contest-winning *William Blake, Not Blessed Angel But Restless Man* (Red Ochre Press, 2014), *Swimming in the Ladle of Stars* (Kattywompus Press, 2014), and *City Of Tents* (Crisis Chronicles Press, 2014). He has seven full-length collections including national award winner for *Searching for What You Cannot See* (Hiraeth Press, 2013), *Before Anything, There Was Mystery* (Flutter Press, 2014), and *Irises, the Lightning Conductor For Van Gogh's Illness* (Aldrich Press, 2014). Forthcoming is *Waiting for the Day to Open Its Wings* (UNBOUND Content), *Martin Willitts Jr, Greatest Hits* (Kattywompus Press), *The Way Things Used To Be* (Writing Knights Press), and *How to Be Silent* (FutureCycle Press). Martin was the winner of the 2012 Big River Poetry Review's William K. Hathaway Award ; co-winner of the 2013 Bill Holm Witness Poetry Contest; winner of the 2013 "Trees" Poetry Contest; winner of the 2014 Broadsided award; winner of the 2014 Dylan Thomas International Poetry Contest. Several of his poems in *Kentucky Review* are based on his visit to Swansea, Wales, to receive the award and read his poem.

Jeffrey Zable is a teacher and conga drummer who plays Afro-Cuban folkloric music for dance classes and Rumbas around the San Francisco Bay Area. He's published five chapbooks including *Zable's Fables* with an introduction by the late great Beat poet Harold Norse. Present or upcoming writing in *Coe Review, On The Rusk, Snow Monkey, After The Pause, Edge, Chrome Baby, Chaos Poetry Review* (featured poet), *The Inflectionist Review, Tule Review* and many others.

Made in the USA
Charleston, SC
07 March 2015